The Knights Templar

in the Holy Land

Dr David West

Cover image

Ein Kreuzritter auf der Wacht im Gebirge

(A Crusader on Watch in the Mountains)

Carl Friedrich Lessing 1808-1880 Düsseldorf School

Städelsches Kunstinstitut und Städtische Galerie, Frankfurt

Cover design and maps by Lawrie Morrisson.

ISBN: 9 781838 071523

 Hamilton House Publishing Ltd

Rochester upon Medway, Kent, UK, ME2 3EA.
Visit hamiltonhousepublishing.com.

In association with

Dedicated to my wife Jenny

for her love, patience and invaluable advice, always.

Other masonic books by Dr David West

Published by Hamilton House Publishing Ltd

The Goat, the Devil, and the Freemason

A shorter history of Goats, Devils, and Freemasons

Things to do when you have nothing to do (3rd edition)
never be short of candidates again

Deism (2nd edition)
at the time of the founders of the Premier Grand Lodge

Managing the Future of Freemasonry (2nd edition)

Masonic Legends, with Matthew West

The Enigma of the Royal Arch

Author Dr David West BA, PhD taught at universities in England and Canada, publishing in the academic press. He worked for Ford and Xerox (President's Award for exceptional service) and was special adviser to a government minister. He founded The Working Manager Ltd, creating the core of its web based management education process. His mother lodge is St Laurence, No. 5511. He is a Mark Master and a Royal Ark Mariner.

Designer Lawrie Morrisson is an engineer by training, and specialised in the design of major public sector electrical installations. Latterly he completed studies in photography and has taken up web design, creating masonic websites in Essex and beyond. His mother lodge is St Laurence, No. 5511. He is a founder and Secretary of the Lodge of Daily Advancement (a lodge committed to learning), an RA mason, and serves on the board of Upminster Masonic Hall Ltd.

Contents - Maps are not to scale and not to be used for navigation!

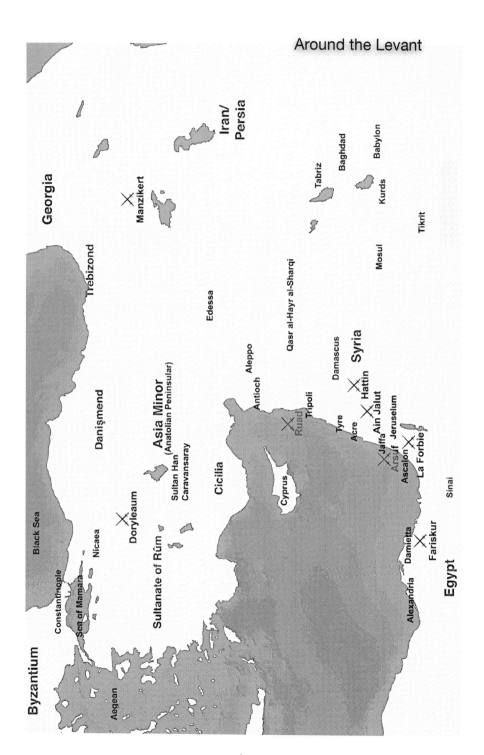

Around the Levant

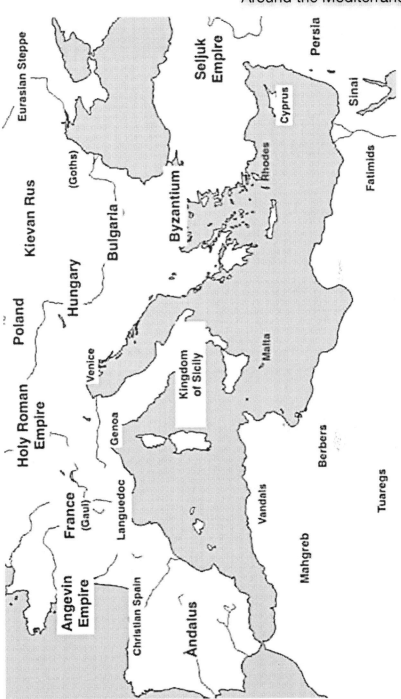

Arabic pronunciation

Arabic has been transcribed into the western alphabet for non-Arabic speakers. Consonants and vowels can be pronounced as in English, but Arabic pronunciation alters this by the use of what are known as *diacritical marks*. For interest, I have shown them where I could find the correct use but, in truth, they will matter only in the highly unlikely event that you read this book aloud to an Arabic speaker.

Vowels marked with line over the top like ā ī ū are long. Thus *jihād* is pronounced *jihard*, *Sunnī* as *sunnee* and *mamlūk* as *mamlook*. The name of the famous *Nūr ad-Dīn* becomes *Noor ad Deen* and the first name of the infamous Saddām Hussein is pronounced *Saddaam*. The first letter of *Saddām* is actually transcribed as Ṣ — note the dot. This changes the pronunciation to a sort of explosive *TS* sound. A dot under a Ḍ does much the same thing, hardening the sound — not *deer* but *ridden*. The name *Riḍwān* thus becomes *Riddwaan*. The dot <u>over</u> the İ in *İstanbul* makes it more like *eestanbul*. In fact, the 2nd syllable is emphasised, thus *eesTANbul*, like *East Stanmore*.

A hyphen or an underscore (the use of which seems to be optional) reminds us to avoid eliding the two parts. Thus the hyphen in the name *Nūr ad-Dīn* reminds us to pronounce both *d* sounds — not *adding* but *add date*. The name of the palace in Granada, the Al Hambra (al-Ḥamrāʾ) is not pronounced *allambra* but *al* (space) *hambra* as in the name of the great Green Bay Packers cornerback *Al Harris*. He is not known as *Alarris*.

The prefix *al-* means *the*, the definite article, often shown in lower case even at the beginning of a sentence. The apostrophe in the middle of a word, as in *Qur'an*, is a glottal stop as in cockney or Essex estuary English where *rattle* become *ra'l*. In *Danişmend* and *Rûm*, the twiddle under the ş alters it to *sh* as in *fish*. The hat over the û changes it to *roum* or *rowm*.

Reading Arabic names

Take the example of <u>Majd al-Din Muhammad ibn Khalid ibn 'Abd
Allah al-Tamimi</u>. *Majd al-Din* is a formal title, provided by state
authorities, this meaning *the glory of religion*. *Muhammad* is a given
name for use only in intimate settings; *ibn* means *son of* (*bint* daughter
of). His father was Khalid and his grandfather was ʿAbd Allah. *al-Tamimi* is an adjective which may describe a birthplace, profession,
sect, or tribe, here meaning *from the tribe of Tamim*.[1]

Glossary

Allāh	The one God, hence *in shā'Allāh* (if God wills).
Asia Minor	Anatolian Peninsula, most of modern Turkey.
Assassins	Ismāʿīlī sect in mountains of Iran and Syria.
Ayyubid	Caliphate (1170-1260) based in Cairo & Damascus.
Atabeg	Turkic leader, subordinate to a monarch.
Basileus	Occasionally used title for Byzantine emperors.
Bosphorus	Strait between Black Sea and Sea of Marmara.
Caliph	Successor to the Prophet, religious leader.
Caliphate	A religious and political entity ruled by a caliph.
Chinggis Khan	12th/13th century Mongol leader.
Crusader	One who *takes the cross* to fight for Christian God.
Dardanelles	Strait between the Sea of Marmara and the Aegean.
Emir	Arabic military commander.
Fa'qih	One skilled in the *fiqh*, social legislation, as opposed to the *sharī'a*, divine law.
Fatimid	Caliphate (909-1171) based in Egypt.
Franj	Arabic for Franks, a term for Crusaders.
Golden Horde	Russian division of Mongol empire.

---

[1] Précis from *The Race for Paradise*, Paul M. Cobb, Oxford University Press, 2014.

iv

Ḥadīth	The Prophet's spoken words, actions or assumed approval.
Horde	From Turkic *ordu* - army or seat of power.
Hospitallers	Order of Knights of the Hospital of Saint John of Jerusalem.
Huns	Tribe terrorising Roman Europe 370-455 CE.
Islām	Muslim faith, or body of believers.
Knightly Order	Templars, Hospitallers, Lazarists, Teutonic Order & others - warrior monks.
Lazarists	Knights of the Order of St Lazarus, originally hospital for care of lepers. The leprous fought.
Levant	Syria, Jordan, Lebanon, Israel, Egypt & Turkey.
Mamlūks	Slave soldiers who became rulers of Egypt.
Mongols	Mounted warriors from between Russia & China.
Ottoman empire	Turkish 1326-1683, named for leader Osman I.
Outremer	Literally *overseas*, settler lands in Levant.
Pilgrims	Travellers to sacred sites.
Qādī	Judge in Islamic civil & religious law.
Rum	Rome & Romans, Byzantium & Byzantines..
Rûm (Sultanate)	Seljuk Asia Minor (Anatolian Peninsula).
Saracens	Islamic Arabs, later all Muslims in Levant.
Settlers	Westerners living in the Levant.
Seljuks	Turkic tribe originating in the Russian Steppe.
Sulṭān	Monarch, subordinate in religion to Caliph.
Türkmen	Generic name for Turkic tribes.
Umayyad	Caliphate (661-750) based in Baghdad & Cordoba.

Dating

Dates in this book are in the modern Gregorian calendar. Years are referred to as BCE (before the common era) and CE (common era). The Islamic (Hijri) calendar begins in the year in which the Prophet left Mecca for Medina. The year 2022 CE is 1443 Hijri.

Timeline

272-337	Emperor Constantine founds Constantinople.
476	Effective end of western Roman empire.
570-632	Life of Muhammad.
632	Rāshidun caliphate.
661-750	Umayyad caliphate.
711	Berbers invade Spain.
750	Abbasid caliphate.
809	Arab empire at its peak: Samarkand to Morocco.
1017	Norman mercenary bands in Mediterranean lands.
1071	Seljuks defeat Byzantines at Battle of Manzikert.
1080	Hospital of St John founded in Jerusalem.
1095	Byzantium appeals for help.
1096	People's crusade.
1097	First crusade.
1099	Crusaders take Jerusalem.
1113	Pope recognises Order of St John (Hospitallers).
c.1118	Templars established.
1129	Pope recognises Order of the Temple.
1137	Birth of Saladin.
1147/1149	Second crusade.
1147	Templars begin to wear white surcoat & red cross.

c.1158	Birth of Genghis Khan.
1176	Saladin proclaimed Sulṭān of Egypt & Syria.
1187	Saladin defeats Crusaders at Ḥaṭṭīn & takes Jerusalem.
1189/92	Third crusade with Richard I & Philip II.
1192	Treaty of Jaffa agreed between Saladin & Richard I.
1193	Death of Saladin.
1199	Death of Richard I.
1202/4	Fourth crusade sacks Byzantium.
1206-1227	Reign of Chinggis Khan.
1218	Fifth crusade attacks Egypt.
1219/20	Chinggis Khan moves westward.
1229	Sixth crusade. Frederick II agrees deal over Jerusalem.
1235-1255	Golden Horde invades Eastern Europe.
1244	Muslims defeat Crusaders at Battle of La Forbie.
1244	Jerusalem taken by mercenaries.
1249	Seventh crusade to Egypt.
1258	Mongols sack Baghdad.
1260	Mamlūk Baibars becomes Sulṭān.
1261	Mamlūks defeat a reduced Mongol army.
1270/72	Eighth crusade to Tunis.
1271	Ninth crusade with future Edward I of England
1291	Mamlūks expel last of Crusaders from mainland.
1302	Mamlūks expel Templars from Ruad.
1312	Templars dissolved.
1317	De Molay burnt at stake.
1797	First Grand Conclave of masonic Knights Templar.

1139   *Omne Datum Optimum* - Innocent II, official recognition of Templars.

1187   *Audita tremendi* - Gregory VIII, calling for the third crusade.

1252   *Ad extirpanda* - Innocent IV, authorising torture to gain confessions from heretics.

1307   *Pastoralis praeeminentiae* - Clement V, ordering arrest of Templars and seizure of their assets.

1308   *Faciens misericordiam* - Clement V, reserving fate of the Templars to the Pope alone.

1312   *Vox in excelso* - Clement V, abolishing Templars.

1312   *Ad providam* - Clement V, granting Templar assets to Hospitallers.

1261   Letter, *Clamat in Auribus* - Alexander IV, on Mongol threat.

The name, *Bull*, is taken from the lead or even gold seal (Latin *bulla*) bearing the name of the Pope. The name was not used before the 13th century although equivalent documents date from the 6th century.

Seal of Pope Innocent IV

Who's who

Abu Shama	13thC. *Book of two gardens* on Nūr al-Dīn & Saladin.
Al-Ashraf Khalil	13th C. 8th Mamlūk Sulṭān who conquered Acre.
Albert of Aix	12th C. historian of 1st crusade.
Alexios Angelos	Deposed Byzantine leader, reneged on deal to re-install him, causing sack of Constantinople.
Alexios I Komnenos	Byzantine leader whose appeal started crusades.
ʿAlī ibn Abī Ṭālib	4th caliph of Rāshidun caliphate, inspired Shi'a.
al-Malik al-Kāmil	Sulṭān, negotiated treaty with Frederick II.
Atâ-Malek Juvayni	1260 *History of World Conqueror* on life of Chinggis.
Bahāʾ ad-Dīn	1200 *Sultany anecdotes and Josephly virtues*, life of Saladin, Joseph being his personal name.
Baibars	4th Mamlūk Sulṭān & general.
Baldwin I	1st official King of Jerusalem.
Baldwin II	2nd King of Jerusalem.
Baldwin of Ibelin	Deserted King of Jerusalem before battle of Ḥaṭṭīn.
Benedict (Saint)	6thC. author of first monastic Rule.
Benjamin of Tudela	12thC. Jewish traveller & author.
Bernard (Saint)	11/12thC. religious leader, author of Templar Rule.
Bohemond I	11thC. Prince of Antioch.
Edward, Lord Herbert of Cherbury	16/17thC. polymath, often called first Deist.
Frederick II	Holy Roman Emperor, led 6th crusade.
Ghâzân Kahn	13thC. Il-Khan, sought Franco-Mongol alliance.
Godfrey de Bouillon	1st ruler of Jerusalem, refused title of king.
Gregory VIII	12thC. Pope, instigator of 3rd crusade.
Guiscard, Robert	& brother Roger, Norman adventurers, Sicily 1260.
Henry II	King of England, father of Richard I.
Honorius III	13thC. Pope, promoted 5th crusade.

Hülegü	13thC. Mongol warlord & 1st Il-Khan.
Ibn 'Abd Az-Zahir	13thC. secretary to Baibars.
Ibn al-Athīr	12th/13thC. scholar, *The Complete History*.
Ibn Jubayr	12th/13thC. geographer & traveller.
Ibn Wāṣil	13thC. *History of the Ayyubids*.
Imad ad-Dīn	12th/13thC. historian of Nūr al-Dīn & Saladin.
Innocent IV	13thC. Pope, sent first emissaries to Mongols.
John	King of England following Richard I.
John of Würzberg	12thC. priest & pilgrim, wrote 'guide book'.
Kilij Arslan I	11th century Seljuk Sulṭān of Rûm.
Louis IX	King of France, led 7th crusade, Saint 1297.
Nūr al-Dīn	Followed Zengī in unifying Muslim forces.
Oliver of Paderborn	11th/12thC. crusader, *History of Damietta*.
Peter the Hermit	Preached disastrous people's crusade.
Philip II	12th/13thC. King of France, 3rd crusade.
Philip IV	14thC. King of France, aimed to abolish Templars.
Prester John	Mythical Christian patriarch.
Qalawūn	13thC. Mamlūk Sulṭān, took Tripoli & besieged Acre.
Raymond III	12thC. Count of Tripoli, treasonably assisted Saladin.
Reynard de Chatillon	12thC. Prince of Antioch, beheaded by Saladin.
Roger of Wendover	13thC. English historian, *Flowers of History*.
Sæwulf	Late 11thC. English pilgrim, wrote *Travels*.
Saladin	12thC. Islamic leader, re-gained Jerusalem 1187.
Urban II	11thC. Pope, set crusades in motion.
William of Tyre	12thC. born Jerusalem, wrote history of city.
Zengī Imad ad-Dīn	12thC. began unification of Muslim forces.

صلاح الدين يوسف بن أيوب

Ṣalāḥ ad-Dīn Yūsuf ibn Ayyūb

ريتشارد

Richard

القُدس

Jerusalem

Introduction

The great historian Steven Runciman needed three volumes, each more than 300 pages long, to describe the crusades. This single volume limits itself to describing the factors and events affecting Templar life during the crusades: their religious status, who they sought to protect, who was there when they arrived, who they fought, and what really brought about their end.

 Unlike the primary forms of Freemasonry, the masonic order of the Knights Templar[1] is restricted to Christians acting in *the name of the Holy, Blessed and Glorious Trinity*. The modern masonic knight symbolically draws his sword against opposers of the gospel, and swears to

love, honour, and fear God; walk after His commandments. Maintain and defend the Christian Faith and [the] honour, dignity and interests of our Order ... Prefer honour to wealth. Be just and true in word and deed. Give no willing cause of offence to any; but, while opposing wrong and injustice, deport himself courteously and gently ... Assist the distressed, eschew all debasing employment, recreation and company; abhor pride and selfishness.

Although there is no historical connection between today's masonic Templars and the Templars of the 12th and 13th centuries, their vows and values do have much in common.

---

[1] The United Religious, Military and Masonic Orders of the Temple and of St John of Jerusalem, Palestine, Rhodes and Malta.

Part one

Setting the Scene

Templar castle at Baghras today.

Understanding the Templars

Jerusalem was captured in 1099, the culmination of the first crusade, but there were no Knights Templar involved. It was nineteen years later in 1118, according to William Archbishop of Tyre,[1] that nine *noble men of knightly Order, devoted to God, pious and God-fearing* took vows before the Patriarch of Jerusalem to protect pilgrims in the Holy Land. Pilgrims had long journeyed there, perhaps as early as 300 CE, welcomed for the income they represented. Numbers increased following the first crusade even though pilgrimage became more dangerous, despite or perhaps because of the capture of Jerusalem. In 1120, out of a party of 700 pilgrims, 300 were killed and 60 enslaved.

The Templar Order received papal recognition in 1129 at the Council of Troyes in the presence of Bernard of Clairvaux (later canonised as St Bernard, but nothing to do with the dog). They were recognised as a Monastic Order. Thus their status differed markedly from that of the ordinary Crusader. The Knights Templar were monks.

When ordinary Crusaders took the cross, they were making an informal and personal commitment to go on a crusade, often through social pressure. In the lead up to the first crusade, the reluctant might be given bits of wool, like the white feathers given by women to civilian men of fighting age in 1914 and 1915. Having taken the cross, if they did not go, and many did not, any sanction would be no more than social.[2] Philip V of France warned a cousin in 1319, that failure to fulfil his crusade promise would provoke *'la honte du monde'*.[3]

---

[1] *Historia rerum in partibus transmarinis gestarum,* A History of Deeds done beyond the Sea, William of Tyre, trnsl. Emily Atwater Babcock & A. C. Krey, Columbia University Press, 1943.

[2] *God's War: A New History of the Crusades,* Christopher Tyerman, Penguin, 2007.

[3] Shame of the world. *How to Plan a Crusade: Reason and Religious War in the High Middle Ages,* Christopher Tyerman, Penguin Books, 2015.

Nevertheless an inquiry in Lincolnshire in England after the Third Crusade found that in twenty out of twenty-nine cases the cause of default was poverty. Some, rich enough, bought their way out. Henry II, father of Richard I, took the cross in 1172, following the murder of Thomas à Becket, and again in 1177, but never went.

> [What] *washed from Henry the guilt of Becket's murder was the supporting of two hundred Knights Templar in Palestine for a year.*[1]

Supporting 200 knights for a year may not sound generous but it was equivalent to the produce of 150,000 acres (60,000 hectares) of farmland, one quarter of the land today owned by the National Trust or about the size of St Lucia in the Caribbean.

The Templar Rule

Unlike the informal commitments of ordinary Crusaders, Templar vows were binding in church law; they were monks in obedience to the Templar Rule. They prayed at the canonical hours,[2] were forbidden distinction in dress, the embrace of women, and personal money. They lived communally, sleeping in a dormitory and taking meals together.

The Rule was based on the Rule of St Benedict *c.*526 CE, with its practice of *ora et labora* (prayer and labour) devoting eight hours to prayer, eight hours to sleep, and eight hours to work, learning and charity. Freemasons will note the similarity to the explanation of the 24 inch gauge in the working tools of an entered apprentice. Rule 340 is similar to today's masonic Templar obligation.

> *Each brother should strive to live honestly and to set a good example to secular people and other orders in everything in such a way that those who see him cannot notice anything bad in his behaviour, not in his*

---

[1] *The History of the Crusades*, Charles Mills, Longman, 1821, Forgotten Books, 2016.

[2] *Matins* (early morning), *Lauds* (following Matins), *Prime* (daylight), *Terce* (9 a.m.), *Sext* (midday), *Nones* (3 p.m.), *Vespers* (sunset), *Compline* (just before bed).

4

riding, nor in his walking, nor in his drinking, nor in eating, nor in his look, nor in any of his actions and work. And especially should each brother strive to conduct himself humbly and honestly when he hears the office of Our Lord.[1]

They did not observe the fasts specified in the monastic calendar. They had to be literally fighting fit, but even on active service, they were expected to take communion.

Being prepared by communion, they should not fear going into battle. Having taken the cup of salvation, they would be avenging the death of Christ by their own.[2]

New type of order

A principle of the monastic life had hitherto been that no monk could shed blood, so the Templar Rule governed a completely new type of religious order, one for monks who promised to *God and to Lady St Mary for all the remaining days of their life, to conquer with all the strength and power that God has given them the Holy Land of Jerusalem.* This is reflected in Rule 57, that *this armed company of knights may kill the enemies of the cross without sinning,* but the conflict between the monastic life and the Templars' military duties ran deep.

(St) Bernard produced a tract[3] to dissipate the qualms of the church and, it must be said, those of the Templars themselves.

This is, I say, a new kind of knighthood ... It ceaselessly wages a twofold war both against flesh and blood and against a spiritual army of evil in the heavens ... He is truly a fearless knight and secure on every side, for his soul is protected by the armour of faith just as his body is protected by armour of steel.

[1] *The Rule of the Templars*, trnsl. J.M. Upton-Ward, Boydell Press, 1992.

[2] *The New Knighthood*, Malcolm Barber, Cambridge University Press, 1994.

[3] *Liber ad milites Templi: De laude novae militae*, ORD Online Encyclopædia.

Nevertheless, following the second crusade Everard des Barres, the pious third Grand Master, abdicated and entered the traditional monastery at Clairvaux to devote *the remainder of his days to the most rigorous penance and mortification.*[1]

Justification

The Crusaders fought a holy war against Islām, an idea that presented and presents obvious difficulties for Christianity, which teaches that men and women must love their enemies.

> *If someone strikes you on one cheek, turn to him the other also. And if someone takes your cloak, do not withhold your tunic.*
>
> 1 Corinthians 7:36.

To overcome this, when preaching the first crusade Pope Urban II, quoted the gospel of Matthew, out of context it must be said.

> *Then said Jesus unto his disciples, 'If any man will come after me, let him deny himself, take up his cross, and follow me.' (16:24)*
>
> *Every one that hath forsaken houses, or brethren, or sisters, or father, or mother, or wife, or children, or lands, for my name's sake, shall receive an hundredfold, and shall inherit everlasting life. (19:29)*

Full remission of sins and eternal life was promised by Pope Gregory VIII in his 1187 bull *Audita tremendi.*

> *Whether they survive or die, they should know that they, after they have made a true confession, will have the relaxation of the penance imposed, by the mercy of almighty God.*

An anonymous preacher put it more bluntly. *He who takes the cross will cross over to the Lord through a shortcut and profitable way.*[2]

---

[1] *The History of the Knights Templar,* Charles Addison, 1866, reprint Hardpress, 2013.

[2] 'Recruiting sermon *c.*1213-1217,' in Jessalyn Bird, Edward Peters, James M. Powell, (eds) *Crusade and Christendom: Annotated Documents in Translation from Innocent III to the Fall of Acre,* 1187-1291, University of Pennsylvania Press, 2017.

On the other side and matching the promises of Pope Gregory, a ḥadīth says of a martyr that *all his sins are forgiven, at the first spurt of his blood, he sees his place in Paradise.*[1] St Bernard may have been sure that the Templars were doing the work of God in eliminating the Saracens who had defiled the holy land,[2] but Saladin was equally sure that the real contamination was Christian.

St Augustine (354-430 CE) had argued that a war could be *just*, with good intent, legitimate authority, proportionate violence and legal cause.[3] The crusades were justified on the grounds that the Holy Land was not the property of the Muslims; that it had been bought for Christianity by Christ's blood. Muslim claims were denied on the grounds of sexual perversion, rejection of Christian missionaries and the persecution of Christians. Nonetheless, a *holy* war, as opposed to a *just* war, was new.

Jonathan Riley-Smith writes that Christian rationalisations

> *of positive violence are based partly on the belief that a particular religious or political system or course of political events is one in which Christ is intimately involved. If the only way to preserve the integrity of his intentions from those who stand in their way is to use force, then this is in accordance with his desires.*[4]

Templar ranks

The Templars are usually partitioned into three ranks: chaplains, knights and sergeants, the latter's many roles uninformatively lumped together. This division probably owes more to the 11th century French bishop and poet, Adalbero of Laon, than to reality. He

---

[1] A ḥadīth records the Prophet's sayings, actions or approval, not his written word. *In their own words: voices of Jihad*, ed. David Aaron, Rand Corporation, 2008.

[2] Bernard was a gut thinker. The theologian of the time was Peter Abelard.

[3] *Contra Faustum Manichaeum*, (Reply to Faustus the Manichaeum) tr. Richard Stathert, in Philip Schaff ed. *The Nicene and Post-Nicene Fathers*, Hendrickson, 1994.

[4] *The Oxford History of the Crusades*, Jonathan Riley-Smith, Oxford Univ. Press, 1999.

described three immutable orders of society: those who pray, those who fight and those who work.

Eligibility to knighthood depended on income, in the twelfth century £40 a year. Templar knights already held that title when recruited, and no one was ever promoted from within. This may sound snobbish but it was Adalbero's immutable order of society at work. There were far fewer Templar knights in the Holy Land than one might think, certainly no more than 600 at any one time. Peter Partner suggests an average of 300,[1] while Runciman[2] estimates 300 at the Battle of Ḥaṭṭīn in a Christian force of 15,000.

The chaplain brothers (*frères chapelains*) had charge of all spiritual matters within the Order: services, confessions, and (most) absolutions. Not part of the normal clerical hierarchy, they answered only to the Pope. The Order was perennially short of *frères chapelains*, which may be why they were treated so well, given the best clothing, food and status at the dining table.

The word translated in English as *sergeant* did not carry the meaning it does today. In medieval Latin the word was *serviens*, carrying the connotation of *serving man*, or *man of service*. In terms of Adalbero's classification, the rank of sergeant is really defined in the negative: they were neither knights nor clerics.

The Templar Rule governed the life of all those who had taken vows to become Templars, and Rule 662 appears to bear out the proletarian nature of a sergeant. It informs a postulant that *he may be told to carry*

---

[1] *The Knights Templar and their Myth*, Peter Partner, Press, 1981.

[2] *History of the Crusades*, Steven Runciman, Cambridge Univ. Press, 1952-1954.

out one of the basest tasks that we have, perhaps at the oven, or the mill, or in the kitchen, or with the camels, or in the pigsty. However, this is a not a description of the roles a sergeant would really be expected to discharge, but more an exhortation to humility, for sergeants came in many forms. Few were what we would consider to be servants, and just about none were non-commissioned officers.

Sergeants formed the great majority of Templars but only some were expected to fight. Non-combatant sergeants were to be found in many, often very significant roles: running the big estates, shipyards, ports, transport, horse and cattle production. Three treasurers of the Paris Temple are known to have been sergeants, effectively bankers to the French crown. Sometimes knights were subordinate to sergeants, for the truth is that knights in general were not much good for anything except fighting.

Many sergeants did perform manual and administrative tasks: farm hands, artisans, administrators, charity workers, and household help,[1] and the 1129 French version of the Rule mentions *frères de mestier* (skilled manual workers, brothers with trades). Some *frères* we know were masons, since rule 325 forbids any brother to wear gloves, except for *mason brothers … because of the great suffering they endure and so that they do not easily injure their hands.*

Of course, sergeants did fight. If you read the Templar Rule, you will find that it is focused on military and religious matters, primarily intended for Templars in the Holy Land. The brother sergeants mentioned in the Rule were genuine soldiers, fighting alongside the Templar knights, although as befitting their place in the social hierarchy they were less well armoured. They were given one horse

---

[1] The Rule also mentions Saracen scribes (perhaps translators), turcopoles (usually indigenous light cavalry) and cooks. Squires, recruited by the knights they served, cared for the war horses and supported their masters on campaign.

instead of the knights' three and when in 1147 the knights began to wear the red cross on a white tunic, they wore it on a black tunic.

The knight and sergeant brothers of the Templar Rule were the heavy cavalry, but the Templars used other fighting sergeants: archers, siege engineers, and sappers. They later recruited sailors whose involvement in fighting was perhaps limited, although they may have fought off pirates and Muslim ships. All of these might, or might not, have been *brother* sergeants.

Brothers or paid hands

It is wrong to assume that all sergeants were volunteers, monks and members of the Templar Order. Many were paid hands, making no religious promises. They usually signed on for a specific length of time or a particular event. The word *mercenary* has a bad connotation, but this is what they were. We can see something of this in the defence of the Order made by Pope Honorius III in 1218. There had been mutterings and complaints about the taxation that helped finance the Templars. Honorius wrote that if the Templars did not *daily spend money for their sergeants, their crossbowmen, and other necessary combatants,* they would be totally incapable of doing what was expected of them.[1]

A *brother* sergeant who took Templar vows would, of course, receive no pay. William of Tyre says that Templars *devoted themselves to the service of Christ, made their vows ... and declared that they wished to live forever in chastity, obedience, and poverty.*[2] Sergeants taking the vows were known as *frères sergeants dou couvent* (brother sergeants of the convent). When the arrests of Templars began in 1308, the majority of

---

[1] 'Pope Honorius III orders prelates of Sicily,' in *The Templars*, trnsl. & ed. Malcolm Barber & Keith Bate, Manchester University Press, 2002.

[2] William of Tyre, *op. cit.*

those arrested were *frères sergeants dou couvent*.[1] Three, known by name, received life sentences.

Deployment

Knights were expensive to maintain and difficult to replace, so the Templar Order was cautious in their deployment. At the Battle of La Forbie in 1244, only one in ten Templar knights survived,[2] so it was rare for them to charge unsupported. A letter written after the 1187 Battle of Ḥaṭṭīn discloses that a*t around the third hour the Master of the Temple charged with all his brothers. They received no assistance, and God allowed most of them to be lost.*[3] The central convent was effectively annihilated.[4]

More had been captured than killed on the field of battle. The Templar Grand Commander told Pope Urban III that 230 captured knights had been beheaded. Leaders could expect to be ransomed but the ordinary knight or sergeant could expect no mercy.

The Templars were highly disciplined. Almost everything in their life was governed by their Rule, both monastic and military. Rules 161 to 163 govern behaviour in squadron, particularly to safeguard the dramatic impact of the charge.

> *When they are established in squadrons, no brother should go from one squadron to another, nor mount his horse nor take up his shield or lance without permission: and when they are armed and they go in squadron … no brother should turn his horse's head towards the back to fight or shout, or anything else.*

---

[1] 'Notes on Templar personnel and government,' Alan Forey, *Journal of Medieval History, 2009.*

[2] 'The Military Orders,' Alan Forey, in Riley-Smith, *op. cit.*

[3] 'Letter to Archumbald,' before 4 September 1187, in *The Conquest of Jerusalem and the Third Crusade, sources in translation,* Peter W. Edbury, Ashgate Publishing 1998.

[4] Forey, in Riley-Smith. *op. cit.*

The command to charge could be given only by the Marshal with the *Gonfalon*, the Piebald Banner (*left*). Guarded by ten knights, it formed a rallying point in the ensuing melée. Templar discipline made them invaluable to crusader leaders in various ways. At the Battle of Arsuf, they held the front rank in Richard's battle formation of five lines, and during his march south after the first siege of Acre in 1191, they collected oxen and fodder, and recovered bodies while beating off Turkish attacks.[1]

Finance

Crusades were cripplingly expensive. In 1180 a knight required *about 30 manses (equivalent to about 300 hectares or about 750 acres) to equip and maintain himself as a mounted warrior. By about 1260 he could not manage on less than 150 manses.*[2] The cost to French King Louis IX of his 1248 crusade (the seventh) was at least six times his annual income, and that does not include the expenses of the great lords and their knights. Crusaders were faced with converting land into ready cash, usually taking a heavy loss on the transaction.

> *Prospective Crusaders seem to have been deeply apprehensive about the long and dangerous journey … but were willing to sell virtually all their possessions to fund their participation.*[3]

Most Crusaders raised sufficient funds to see them through but many others ran out, and during the third crusade, Richard I paid for impoverished knights himself. Money was a constant source of

---

[1] Barber, *op. cit.*

[2] Barber, *op. cit.*

[3] *The Crusades*, Thomas Asbridge, Simon & Schuster, 2010.

worry to all Crusaders, as Richard I wrote in an 1191 letter to the Abbot of Clairvaux.

> *The Duke of Burgundy, with the French under his command, and Count Henry with his men and the other counts, barons and knights have spent all their wealth in the service of God and will return to their own lands unless by the ingenuity of your preaching thoughtful provision may be made … for more money to be spent in God's service.*

The financial burden may account for the constant desire for plunder and pillage, but crusades were not self-financing. Although the quantities of booty could be spectacular, they rarely outweighed expenditure.[1]

Supply

The Templars had little interest in plunder. They were supported from the proceeds of their estates, donated to the Order for the remission of sins. One Pons Lautier granted lands to the Templars, *so that God and our Lord Jesus Christ may give me and my parents remission for our sins and grant us access to the heavenly kingdom.*[2]

Logistical support was provided by the Order's 15,000 members, men and women, managing the 9,000 Templar estates. Most were essentially civilians, doing vitally important work. Without the constant re-supply of men and matériel from Europe, the Templars would not have survived even one major defeat. Major N. R. M. Borton, in his case study *The 14th Army in Burma*,[3] writes of the importance of effective logistics. He says of General William Slim[4] in the Burma campaign:

---

[1] *English Society and the Crusade, 1216-1307*, Simon Lloyd, Clarendon Press, 1988.

[2] 'The pilgrimage of Pons Lautier of Colonzelle,' in Barber & Bate, *op. cit.*

[3] 'The 14th Army in Burma,' Major N. R. M. Borton, *Defence Studies*, autumn 2002.

[4] Later 1st Viscount Slim.

The magnitude of the logistic task facing Slim when he assumed command of the 14th Army must have appeared insurmountable. He was fully aware of its importance: 'I knew that the campaign in Burma would above all be a supply and transport problem.' Furthermore ... as he advanced south through Burma, he knew that his logistic problems would increase as his lines of communication extended.

The same could be said of the task in the Holy Land. Slim's logistics were managed by Major-General 'Grocer Alf' Snelling, a man of exceptional ability, and the Templars' logistics had to be handled equally well, not only in quantity but in timing. Any interruption could be fatal.

While the overriding purpose of the supply chain was to provide for the front, there were obviously overheads. Estate workers had to be paid, fed and clothed. Buildings had to be maintained. Tools had to be provided, taxes and charitable donations paid. Ten percent of bread produced was given to the poor. Pensions were substantial, a cost increasing over time. By 1318, pensions were being paid to former Templars in France, England, Ireland, Belgium, Germany, Italy, Cyprus, and Spain.[1]

Horses

The Templar Order maintained over four thousand horses in *Outremer,* with mules and camels in addition. Despite Matthew Paris's famous 1250 CE drawing, Templar Rule 379 makes it clear that *two brothers should not ride on one horse.* The average price of horses tripled between 1140 and

---

[1] Barber, *op.cit.*

1180, doubling again by 1220, so the Templars took great care of them. Other knights would ask Templars to treat their sick animals.

A mounted knight was not impregnable, although his armour and speed gave him a great advantage. Not until the 15th century did knights appear in the shining armour depicted in many a romantic painting.[1] The crusader knight was protected by chain mail, good against swords if not against crossbows or longbows, but his horse was his real weak point. If his horse was killed under him, he became just another infantry soldier. Abū Shāma remarks that many knights were captured but *there were no horses amongst the spoils*.[2]

Trading Nava, this one lateen rigged.

Thus, as early as 1123, a maritime delivery system of horse transports was developed, using sailing ships and galleys equipped with landing ramps. *Naves*, lateen or square rigged sailing ships, were the most efficient cargo carriers, requiring a small crew, if not quite the man, boy and dog of the Norfolk wherry. The standard galley was a bireme (two banks of oars), 40 metres overall with 108 oarsmen. Its advantage was its consistent speed and windward ability but its disadvantage was the huge crew and resultant limit on cargo space.

---

[1] *A Knight and his Armour*, Ewart Oakshott, Dufour, 2nd ed. 1999. In the destruction of yet another fondly held myth, he declares that knights never had to be hoisted onto their horses by cranes. The weight of later full plate armour was only about 57 lbs (25 kg), and a trained knight could easily mount and remount on his own.

[2] *The Book of the Two Gardens*, quoted in Sir Hamilton Gibb in *The Life of Saladin*, Clarendon Press, 1973.

Forage and water

It was not only horses that had to be delivered to the Levant; forage mattered too. The *destriers* or great horses used in tournaments were massive, weighing over 2,000 pounds, but were not fast nor nimble enough for combat. *Coursers,* highly trained horses of about 1,000 pounds weight, were used by knights, while sergeants-at-arms usually rode *rounceys,* general riding horses.[1] Sarah Evers Conrad estimates that a 1,000-pound horse in light work consumes twenty pounds of forage – grass or hay – every day. It also consumes five to ten gallons of water, typically half a gallon for every pound of hay.[2] The exercise, heat, and humidity in *Outremer* increased the need for forage and water up to four times the normal amount.

While Templars always sought to graze their horses, grazing land was not widespread in the Levant.[3] The coast of what is now Lebanon is fertile but further south and inland towards Jerusalem the terrain increasingly becomes arid. Two seasons dominate: a cool, rainy winter and a dry, hot summer, with no rain to speak of from April to October. Winter rainfall is unpredictable: days of drizzle or a fierce downpour causing flooding. As the first crusade marched south from Constantinople, it crossed the Anatolian plateau, noted for its extremely hot, dry summers and cold wet winters.

Income

Clarence Perkins researched Templars' holdings in England as at 1312. He estimates that there were 144 Templar members and employees, of whom 20 were knights. They produced an annual income of about £4720, at a time when the annual pay of a knight was about £36, a sergeant £12, and an archer £6.

---

[1] *A Knight and his Horse,* Ewart Oakeshott, Dufour editions, 1999.

[2] 'Horse Feeding Basics,' Sarah Evers Conrad, *The Horse,* December 2019.

[3] Saladin hired bandits to steal grazing horses.

Harlech Castle cost about £8,000.

Estates specialised; some were arable and others stock farms.

The inventories of Bruer, Aslakeby, Eycle and Wylughton [in Lincolnshire] *show that the Templars had thirty-eight sacks, sixteen stone of wool stored away.*[1]

A sack of wool was 26 stone and a wool stone was 16 pounds. In metric, they had stored 7,286 kgs or 7.2 metric tonnes of wool.

At Bruer, the grade 1 listed tower still stands, the remains of the 1185 Temple Bruer preceptory. At Aslakeby, now spelt Aslackby, nothing remains of the c.1164 preceptory, probably at Temple Farm on Temple Road. At Eycle, now Eagle, earthworks remain. At Wylughton, now Willoughton, Temple Garth farm marks the site of the preceptory (built pre-1164).

Fiscal agents

Through their skill in managing estates and finance, the Templars became wealthy, a long way from their initial title, *Poor Knights of Christ*. They soon became bankers. Their 'branch offices' meant that

---

[1] 'The Wealth of the Knights Templars in England,' Clarence Perkins, *American Historical Review*, 1910.

they could make specie, coins and precious metals, available where needed, reducing the dangers of carrying valuables on a journey.

An extreme example of their ready money is the ransom for Louis IX of France. When he was captured in Egypt in 1250 during the seventh crusade, the ransom for his release was immense, variously expressed as one million *dinars*, 800,000 *bezants*[1] or 400,000 *livres tournois*, the amount being one quarter of the King's annual revenue. Half had to be paid immediately but the King came up short. The balance came from a Templar ship lying off the Egyptian coast.

Templars acted as agents for the crown, as in the case of the 40,000 marks entrusted to them by Falkes de Breaute, the Norman adventurer who rebelled against Henry III. *In 1226, the masters of the Order in both France and England were directed to sequestrate this sum as an indemnity for his depredations.*[2] King John (1166-1216) deposited the English crown jewels with the Templars, perhaps *for* security, or perhaps *as* security, because he borrowed extensively from them. The order was often entrusted with deeds, wills and mortgage pledges, gold, silver, and jewels. A document acknowledges the return of

> *all and every jewel that we had deposited and put in safe keeping in the house of the Temple at Monzón* [in Aragon]. *Wherefore we declare the house of the Temple and all the brothers freed from all claims from us and ours concerning all the said jewels.*[3]

During the reigns of Henry III and Edward I of England (1216 to 1307) the Templars served as the royal treasury. Popes also used their services, shown in a letter from Honorius III to the Bishop of Albano.

---

[1] A *bezant* was a Byzantine coin used throughout the Levant and containing 4.5 grams of gold. A Baibar *dinar* was designed to be equivalent but contained 4.25 grams of gold, the average weight of a *bezant* in use.

[2] 'The Financial Relations of the Knights Templar to the English Crown,' Eleanor Ferris, *American Historical Review*, October 1902.

[3] 'Deposit of jewels by James I of Aragon at Monzón,' in Barber & Bate, *op.cit.*

We have also ordered payment from the tax collected in England of thirteen thousands marks, to be handed over to you by our beloved sons [names four men] brothers of the Temple, with the firm intention of sending you the rest quickly.

The Hospitallers and Templars of Hungary have received from the tax raised in Hungary one thousand seven hundred and eleven silver marks and thirty-eight gold marks ... They should receive more when the accounts have been rendered to the chaplain and we have given orders that all these sums shall be sent across the sea to you.[1]

As Eleanor Ferris wrote,

In the unwarlike atmosphere of the counting-room, the soldiers of the Temple, for over a century, handled much of the capital of western Europe, becoming expert accountants, judicious administrators, and pioneers in that development of credit and its instruments, which was destined to revolutionise the methods of commerce and finance.[2]

Clearly the Templars were considered honest and dependable. If, as they were later accused, they were riddled with vice, it seems strange that the kings, popes, lords and ladies who used their services for so many years, did not notice.

Chivalry and violence

Violence was the predominant way of settling disputes and, after agriculture, the main employer. Jennifer Goodman Wollock calls the knights of the day *hired thugs*[3] and the first crusade was partly an attempt by the Pope to give them someone in common to fight. So reasons for taking the cross ranged from the pious to the grubby:

---

[1] 'Gathering crusading taxes (24 July 1220),' in Barber & Bate, *op.cit.*

[2] Ferris, *op. cit.*

[3] *Rethinking Chivalry and Courtly Love*, Praeger Series on the Middle Ages, 2011.

- To visit the greatest of all relics, the land Christ trod.
- To avenge Christ for the insults he received from Islām.
- To reduce the time spent in purgatory.
- To avoid the punishments of hell.
- To enhance personal reputation.
- From fear of shame.
- From obedience to their lord.
- To gain land and title.
- Plunder and booty.
- Travel and a good punch-up.

Gershon argues[1] that chivalry was invented to reduce thuggery.

[1] Livia Gershon, *History.com*, January 2019.

> [Today] *the word 'chivalry' evokes a kind of old-fashioned male respect for women. But during the Middle Ages, the code was established for much grittier reasons. At a time of routine military violence with massive civilian casualties, chivalry was an effort to set ground rules for knightly behaviour.*

The chivalric code was an idealised perfection of bravery, honour, self-deprecation, and courtesy to friend and foe, combined with good manners, urbanity and gallantry towards ladies. The common picture is of the knight in the lists begging a lady's garland or kerchief to grace his lance. Beginning in the 12th century with troubadour poems and songs known as the *Chansons de Geste*, chivalric literature reached its peak in Malory's 14th century *Le Morte d'Arthur* with its stories of King Arthur and the Round Table - but chivalry did not feature in early tournaments.

> *In its most straightforward, but to us perhaps least attractive, form the tournament consisted of a single event involving two large opposing groups of knights who fought each other at some agreed upon place and time … There was frequently no predetermined boundary to the combat area and fighting might range across considerable tracts of country and even through the streets of nearby towns and villages … The fighting in a tournament could be fierce, bloody … and virtually without rules.*[1]

Such violence was seen again in the capture of Jerusalem in 1099.

> *Our men seized great numbers, both men and women, either killing them or keeping them captive … the slaughter was so great that our men waded in blood up to their ankles.*[2]

---

[1] *Tudor and Jacobean Tournaments*, Alan Young, Sheridan House, 1987.

[2] *Gesta Francorum*, Anon, in *The First Crusade: Accounts of Eyewitnesses and Participants*, August C. Krey, reprinted by Forgotten Books, 2016.

In a horror reminiscent of modern times, the Crusaders made the surviving Saracens, of whom there could have been but few, pile bodies of the dead outside the city and burn them to reduce the stench. Of course, if anyone genuinely thought and acted like a Crusader today, they would be thought criminally insane, but the society of the time was almost unimaginably different.

Manners

The personal habits and manners of Crusaders often shocked Muslims. Their bravery and martial prowess drew admiration but their eating habits, drunkenness, intermittent hygiene, lack of medical knowledge, and relations with women, were deemed quite intolerable. We can contrast such behaviour with that of the Templars. Their Rule covered not only what they might eat but also how. They were ordered to eat in pairs to ensure that each ate properly, not affected by *harshness of life or secret abstinence*.

They were allowed wine *at the disposition and judgment of the master*, mixed with water because *wine makes even the wise renounce God*. There was some concern for hygiene because a rule stated that *no brother may bathe, let blood, take medicine, go into town, or ride a horse without permission*. They had rules on clothing, one that *because of the great intensity of the heat which exists in the East, from Easter to All Saints ... a linen shirt shall be given to any brother who wishes to wear it*.

Married brethren were allowed but it was considered *unjust that married brothers remain in one and the same house with brothers who profess chastity to God*. Otherwise they considered it *dangerous to befriend women because the old enemy has cast out many people from the right path of paradise by female companionship*.

Female Crusaders

Despite these Templar admonitions, there is evidence that women fought in the crusades, *to the admiration of western sources and the fascinated horror of Arabic ones.*[1] They were not Templars and the numbers were not large but they are well attested.

In a list of 47 Cornish folk taking the cross, four were women. Ibn al-Athīr[2] wrote that at Acre three captured knights were found to be women only when they removed their coats of mail. Hosler records two Christian defenders at Acre celebrated for their courage, one *a female archer, who wounded several attackers with her bow until she herself was struck down.*[3]

The most famous female Crusader was Margaret of Beverley, described in an account by Thomas of Froidmont, her brother.[4] She is said to have reached Jerusalem in 1187 just after the battle of Ḥaṭṭīn and before Saladin besieged the city. She is described as fighting on the walls of Jerusalem and later at Antioch.

Next

Not all crusades were equally important. The next section will review those most relevant to an understanding of the Templars in the Holy Land.

[1] Tyerman, *God's War, op. cit.*

[2] Ibn al-Athīr, *Perfect History*, ed. D.S. Richards, Routledge, 2006.

[3] *The Siege of Acre 1189-1191*, John D. Hosler, Yale University Press, 2018.

[4] *The Crusades: a reader*, S.J. Allen & Emilie Amt (eds), Univ. of Toronto Press, 2014.

The significant crusades

It is worth keeping in mind that the crusades were only a part of the history of Europe and the Middle East. Life and politics in western Europe were not suspended during the crusading period. The Holy Roman Emperors were in constant dispute with the papacy. Frederick the Great was trying to unite over 1,500 small states, herding cats. His successor, Henry VI, pursued a claim to the kingdom of Naples and Sicily, while his opponents encouraged revolts back home. Louis VI (*le Gros*) of France spent his time either fighting his own barons or at war with the English. His successor was failing to produce a male heir. When Richard I departed on crusade in 1190, his brother John sought to seize the government.

The late 11th century was a time of acute insecurity in Islām. Some Muslims expected a revival of the faith with the ending of the 5th Islamic century. Others awaited the appearance of the Mahdi, the rightly guided one, and the end of the world.

> *Whatever people were expecting it was not a religiously inspired invasion of peoples from western Europe.*[1]

The first crusade

The telling of crusade stories usually begins in 1095 with the Byzantine Emperor, Alexios I Komnenos, calling for help from the Western powers against invading Turks. His appeal was for no more than a small mercenary force to reinforce his own army, but in response Pope Urban II went far beyond Alexios's request and preached the first crusade, admonishing Christians to take up arms to capture the Holy Land for Christ.

---

[1] 'Islām and the crusades, 1096-1699', Robert Irwin, in Riley-Smith, *op. cit.*

It had nothing to do with the Templars, of course. They were not formed until after the end of the crusade, and then only to protect pilgrims on the roads around Jerusalem.

The response to Urban's preaching amazed everyone and two very different groups took the cross, as Guibert, Abbot of Nogent-sous-Coucy, wrote.

> *While the princes, who felt the need of large funds and the support of numerous followers, were making preparations carefully and slowly, the common people, who were poor in substance but abundant in numbers, attached themselves to a certain Peter the Hermit.*[1]

This People's crusade, setting out in April 1096, was no organised body but a mass movement variously led, with Peter the Hermit and Gautier Sans-Avoir the best known leaders. *Pierre l'Ermite* was a priest from Amiens and not altogether an estimable one. It is said that Jesus appeared to him, ordering him to preach the crusade, which he did in his own inflammatory way. He reached Jerusalem, returned home and died in about 1131. Gautier was the minor lord of Boissy-sans-Avoir, a village 50 kms west of Paris. He led a small contingent of knights. Albert of Aix wrote that he died *pierced by seven arrows which had penetrated his coat of mail* in October 1096 at Nicæa, never reaching Jerusalem.

The People's crusade was a very mixed bag, composed of

> *the chaste as well as the sinful, adulterers, homicides, thieves, perjurers, and robbers; indeed, every class of the Christian profession, nay, also and those influenced by the spirit of penance.*[2]

This mass set out first; perhaps 45,000 men, women and children, having no idea of what to expect but devoutly and mistakenly

---

[1] *Dei gesta per Francos, op.cit.*

[2] Albert of Aix, a canon of Aix-la-Chapelle writing in the 12th century. Krey, *op. cit.*

believing that the Holy Ghost would protect them. For them, the Holy Land was just somewhere in the Bible, a place of prophets, miracles, plagues and floods, of myths and legends. Poorly armed, some with no more than a cross sewn on their tunic, they ravaged their way across Europe. Encouraged by Peter, they murdered Jews along the Rhine and Danube, pillaged villages and towns, and generally made a thoroughgoing nuisance of themselves. Many fell by the wayside, dying of sickness and starvation, or killed by the inhabitants of countries they bedevilled.

Arriving in Byzantium, much reduced in number, they were tired, cold, hungry, quarrelling amongst themselves, and disappointed in a God who failed to provide for them. Unable to provision themselves, they stole what they could and *even tore down and burned buildings of the city and carried off the lead with which the [roofs of the] churches were constructed and sold it* [back] *to the Greeks.*[1] The Emperor, enraged by their behaviour, pushed them across the strait of Bosphorus as quickly as he could.

They advanced on the city of Nicæa whose walls were 6,000 metres in length, incorporating 240 turrets. Its Sulṭān, Kilij Arslan, was a young man of 17 but already experienced in warfare. His army fell upon the rabble. Few escaped.

> *The youngest women were kidnapped by the Sulṭān's horsemen and distributed to the emirs or sold in the slave markets. Several young boys suffered a similar fate. The rest ... probably nearly twenty-thousand of them, were exterminated.*[2]

Luck

Kilij Arslan thought he had annihilated an invading army. So intoxicated was he with his success that he disregarded news from

---

[1] *The crusades through Arab eyes*, Amin Maalouf, Saqi Books, 1984.
[2] *Ibid.*

Constantinople that another group was about to cross the Bosphorus. He had beaten the *Franj* once, and saw no reason why he could not do so again.

> *The Sulṭān felt it was time to return to the major preoccupations of the hour — in other words, to the merciless struggle he had long been waging against other Turkish princes, his neighbours. It was there, and nowhere else, that his fate and that of his realm would be decided. The clashes with the Rum or with their foreign Franj auxiliaries would never be more than an interlude.*[1]

He especially coveted the Anatolian lands of the mysterious Danişmend Gazi,[2] and the battle for his castle of Malaṭya was already engaged when a messenger arrived with news that a new *Franj* army had arrived at the gates of Nicæa. Kilij Arslan agreed a truce with Danişmend, not unusual in the Turks' way of internecine fighting, and was able to get home in time, as he thought, to beat the *Franj* as easily as before. Too late he realised that this was not the rabble of his previous encounter, but an army of well-armed professional soldiers already erecting siege engines.

Nevertheless, his own army was no bunch of provincial amateurs. It had, after all, frightened the Byzantine emperor sufficiently to cause him to seek help from the West, but his initial attack was roundly beaten off. Seeking to re-group, he left his city to the invaders, but when the Crusaders came to enter Nicæa, they found it had already surrendered to the emperor.

The Crusaders were both elated and disappointed. They had avoided a punishing attack on the city's walls, but had no opportunity for the pillage they desired.

---

[1] Maalouf, *op. cit.*

[2] Hero of the 13th century Turkic language epic, *The Exploits of King Danishmend.* He is mysterious in that no one really knows much about him.

Fear and suffering

Continuing their march, the Crusaders overcame an ambush Kilij Arslan laid in the valley of Dorylæum. He fled again, telling a squadron of cavalry riding to his help that the *Franj* were too numerous and too powerful for anyone to stop them.[1] These victories were followed by another at Heraclea where, although seriously weakened by lack of water while crossing the Anatolian Plateau, the Crusaders defeated an army under Danişmend. It is said that the sight of a comet illuminated the victory.[2]

The Crusaders marched on Antioch, a fortified city near the sea, whence the governor had expelled Christian inhabitants to prevent them providing entry for the invaders. A siege was set but the besiegers' supplies ran short and starvation loomed. Just in time the governor's preparations proved insufficient and a traitor opened a window. Come night, there was no living Turk in Antioch, just corpses rotting in the summer heat.

This slaughter added to the fear becoming rife throughout the Levant, further intensified by the incident at Ma'arra, a city with only an armed militia for its defence. The citizens had surrendered in the hope that the *Franj* would spare them, but a massacre, and worse, ensued. Fulcher of Chartres wrote, *many of our people, harassed by the madness of excessive hunger, cut pieces from the buttocks of the Saracens already dead there, which they cooked.*[3] Rumours of such cannibalism further reduced the resistance of cities in the path of the Crusaders' march. They competed with gifts of food, horses and jewels to persuade the Crusaders to pass them by.

---

[1] Maalouf, *op. cit.*

[2] Runciman, *op. cit.* The Anglo-Saxon Chronicle records the appearance of a comet in October 1097, *an uncommon star, shining in the evening, and soon hastening to set. It was seen south-west, and the ray that stood off from it was thought very long, shining south-east.* It was not Halley's comet which had appeared 31 years before, in 1066.

[3] Krey, *op. cit.*

It was owing to the jealousies of the Moslem leaders and their refusal to work together that the First Crusade had achieved its object.[1]

The Crusaders' own suffering was very real. The journey was long, some 2000 miles (3334 kms). They faced constant hunger and thirst as their enemy employed scorched earth tactics with poisoned wells. Half the army deserted and one in seven starved to death, but they took Jerusalem, and Christians held it for 88 years.

Time passes. Qāḍī al-Faḍl, a Muslim chronicler of Saladin's time, reports that the unbelievers had *transformed* [it] *into a Paradise garden ... on every side houses as pleasant as their gardens and bright with white marble and columns decorated with leaves, which make them look like living trees.*[2]

Following the first crusade, four Christian states were created, collectively known as *Outremer* (overseas): the counties (ruled by a Count) of Edessa and Tripoli, the principality of Antioch and the kingdom of Jerusalem.

Second crusade

The second crusade (1147-1150) was motivated by the loss of Edessa to Turkic forces. It failed because the French and German armies could not work together, although Bernard of Clairvaux (St Bernard) firmly placed the blame on the sins of the Crusader knights.[3]

What then, O knights, is this ... unbearable urge which bids you fight with such pomp and labor, and all to no purpose except death and sin?

You cover your horses with silk, and plume your armour with I know not what sort of rags; you paint your shields and your saddles; you

---

[1] Runciman, *op. cit.* The Crusaders would often wait out Muslim attacks, expecting their attackers to be called away to defend their own city.

[2] In *Monastic Reform, Catharism, and the Crusades 900-1300*, Bernard Hamilton, Variorum, 1979.

[3] *Liber ad milites Templi, op. cit.*

adorn your bits and spurs with gold and silver and precious stones, and then in all this glory you rush to your ruin with fearful wrath and fearless folly.

The only significant event in this crusade was an attack on Damascus. The Crusaders were successful at first, defeating the defenders' army outside the city and preparing siege works, but the Muslims' call for help was answered by Turkoman cavalry and al-Biqā[1] archers who penned the Crusaders in their camp. Falling out over who should have Damascus when it was won, something looking less and less likely by the minute, and hearing of more Islamic reinforcements, the Crusaders withdrew.

John of Würzberg spread the rumour that the Templars had been bribed by the Muslims to persuade the Holy Roman Emperor to raise the siege.[2] Ralph, Abbot of Coggeshall in Essex, made the same claim in his *Chronicon Anglicanum*,[3] and the anonymous *Chronique d'Ernoul et Bernard le Trésorier*[4] added the Hospitallers to the accusation. William of Tyre generalised the criticism to *certain of our nobles*.[5]

The failures of the second crusade, the search for someone to blame, and the re-capture of Jerusalem by Saladin in 1187, motivated the **third crusade** (1189-1191). It was successful in regaining some coastal cities. A treaty left Jerusalem in Islamic hands but enabled pilgrims to visit freely. (This crusade will be discussed later.)

---

[1] A valley in East Lebanon, now famed for its wine.

[2] *Description of Jerusalem*, trnsl. Aubrey Stewart, Palestine Pilgrims Text Society 1890. Reprint Alpha Editions, 2019.

[3] The remains of Ralph's abbey now form part of the little St Nicholas church, administered by St Peter Ad Vincula in Coggeshall.

[4] *c*.1230. Latrie, Count Louis de Mas ed., *Société de l'histoire de France*, 1871.

[5] 'The Templar Order: A Failed Ideal?' Sophie Menache, *The Catholic Historical Review*, January 1993.

The disastrous fourth

The fourth crusade (1202-1204) was an unmitigated horror. Aimed at Egypt as a back door to the Levant, it was diverted by finance and politics to attack two Christian cities: first sacking Zara (in modern Croatia) as payment to Venice for transport, then attacking Constantinople to re-install Alexios Angelos on the throne of Byzantium. He refused or was unable to pay the 200,000 silver marks he had promised, so the Crusaders (not all in agreement) destroyed *the greatest city in Christendom.*

> [They reduced it to] *a smouldering ruin; its palaces and the great houses of its leading families pillaged, hangings and glorious wardrobes torched, roofs gutted by fire. Entire libraries of documents within, if not already burned, were exposed to rain, food for insects and rodents.*[1]

The Pope was furious, castigating his legate in no uncertain terms.

> *It was your duty to attend to the business of your legation and to give careful consideration, not to the capture of the Empire of Constantinople, but rather to the defence of what is left of the Holy Land and, with the Lord's leave, the restoration of what has been lost … How is the Greek church to be brought back into ecclesiastical union and to a devotion for the Apostolic See when she … sees in the Latins only an example of perdition and the works of darkness … under what guise can we call upon the other Western peoples for aid to the Holy Land and assistance to the Empire of Constantinople?*[2]

Relations between the churches of Rome and Constantinople had been uneasy for some time, and the fourth crusade ended any hope

---

[1] *Byzantium*, Judith Herrin, Princeton University Press, 2009.

[2] 'Pope Innocent III, Epistle 136,' trnsl. James Brundage, *The Crusades: A Documentary History*, Marquette University Press, 1962.

of reconciliation.[1] There is no mention of the Templars in contemporary accounts, and one hopes they were not involved.

Fifth & messy crusade

If the fourth was a horror, the fifth (1217-1221) was a mess. A fleet of perhaps 300 ships left Vlaardingen (near modern Rotterdam) by way of Dartmouth in south-west England, bound for the Levant. Storms dispersed the ships, but most gathered together at Lisbon.

Modern Alcácer do Sal with castle above the city.

The Crusaders were persuaded to attack the Muslim city Alcácer do Sal by the unlikely tale that the Saracens were required to send 1,000 heads of Christians to the King of Morocco each year. The Templars led the successful assault. An anonymous cleric wrote

> *The Saracens trusted their strength, the Christians their faith … the number of captives was infinite … while the captives were being led through the army, they were asking about the signs of the victors, a shining battle line, wearing red crosses.*[2]

---

[1] Pope John Paul II apologised for the event in 2004.

[2] 'The Rhineland Crusaders,' in Jessalynn Bird, *op.cit*. Only Templars wore red crosses.

After further inconsequential raids and more storms the fleet finally reached Acre, where nothing of consequence occurred. King Andrew of Hungary had already arrived but his manoeuvrings had come to little. He was collecting relics.

They were the favoured booty of Crusaders and were big business, fakes becoming a real problem. A joke about John the Baptist's skull was told even then. A pilgrim visiting shrines in France was shown the Baptist's skull on two consecutive days at two different places, the first version being smaller than the second. On being challenged, the quick thinking keeper of the second shrine replied, *The one you saw yesterday was obviously his skull as a young man.*[1]

With the arrival of reinforcements from the Netherlands the crusade was re-aimed at Egypt, the leaders wanting to believe rumours of the imminent arrival of the legendary (and fictitious) Prester John, the first mention of whom had occurred during the second crusade. Benjamin of Tudela wrote,

> *About that time news had reached Europe that a powerful Christian king named Prester John, who reigned over a people coming from Central Asia, had invaded Western Asia and inflicted a crushing defeat upon a Moslem army. Pope Alexander III conceived the hope that a useful ally could be found in this priest-king, who would support and uphold the Christian dominion. He dispatched his physician Philip on a mission to this mysterious potentate to secure his help against the Mohammedans. The envoy never returned.*[2]

The Crusader force landed near Damietta on the Nile Delta coast but as they sought to advance on Cairo the defenders opened sluice gates to flood the land. A glutinous description is given by Oliver of Paderborn.

---

[1] *Strange Landscape*, Christopher Frayling, BBC Books, 1995.

[2] *The Itinerary of Benjamin of Tudela*, trnsl. Marcus Nathan Adler, Feldheim, 1907.

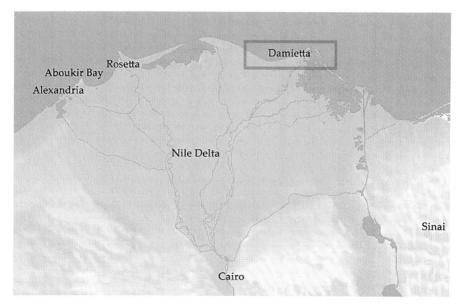

The superabundance of water, following the declivity of the reservoirs through conduits, softened the earth, made dry by long drought, into sticky mud which held tight the horses' hooves; it made the open space of the fields quite impassable.[1]

The Templars made attempts to ensure the destitute received enough food to continue, but facing disease and starvation, the Crusader army surrendered. Oliver provides a religious explanation. Those events favourable to the Crusaders, whom he terms *pilgrims*, resulted from divine intervention.

On the first of May a great multitude of pilgrims began to withdraw, leaving us in the greatest danger. But our kind and merciful Father, our leader and comrade in arms, Jesus Christ ... did not permit the unbelievers to rush in upon us until new and recent pilgrims arrived with abundant aid; a supply of the faithful.

Those unfavourable, resulted from human vices.

No one can describe the corruption of our army after Damietta was

---

[1] 'The capture of Damietta,' Oliver of Paderborn, in Jessalynn Bird, *op. cit.*

given to us by God ... Lazy and effeminate, the people were contaminated with chamberings and drunkenness, fornications and adulteries, thefts and wicked gains.

Frederick II & the sixth crusade

The sixth crusade was instigated by a fishmonger from Uxbridge who saw an apparition.

The Lord showed himself in the sky as when crucified; for on a most shining cross there appeared the body of our Lord pierced with nails and with a lance, and sprinkled with blood.[1]

Apparently this display was a divine complaint against Frederick II, then Holy Roman Emperor. He had delayed his journey to the Holy Land, ostensibly because of ill health, just when an army arrived, ready to fight with him. With no one to lead them, the soldiers went home. The Pope, disappointed with Frederick's dilettante mien, excommunicated him. Technically this meant he could not lead a crusade, so when he did arrive in Acre in 1228, he was welcomed by the Templars but denied the usual kiss of peace. As a monastic body under the Pope's jurisdiction, they were in a quandary. In the end they supported his campaign, but only when he agreed to have his name removed from official orders.

A fascinating figure, Frederick was fluent in Arabic and five[2] other languages. He had a Muslim bodyguard, wore a robe adorned with Arabic symbols, and kept up a regular correspondence with Muslim scientists, unaffected by his deportation of a large number of troublesome Muslims to Apulia in Italy, when King of Sicily. His arrival in the Holy Land with just 3,000 troops meant that he put

---

[1] 'How a great stir was made at this time to assist in the crusade,' Roger Wendover, in Jessalynn Bird, *op. cit.*

[2] Latin, Sicilian, High German, Occitan (the language of Languedoc) and Greek.

diplomacy ahead of force of arms.[1] In 1229, he successfully negotiated a ten year treaty with the Ayyubid Sulṭān al-Malik al-Kāmil. Christians regained Jerusalem except for the Temple Mount, the site of Muhammad's ascent to heaven, the *Mi'raj,* with its Dome of the Rock and al-Aqṣā mosque. The Christians also retained a coastal strip with an isolated Antioch *(red areas).*

A bit more was gained for a couple of years by the Barons' crusade, 1239–1241 *(pink areas),* but in 1244 Khwarazmian mercenaries sacked

---

[1] It has been argued that Frederick meant to use his army to force the Christians to acknowledge him as ruler of the Crusader states. Brundage, *op. cit.* If so, he failed.

Jerusalem. The Templar Grand Master had opposed Frederick's deal on the grounds that it made protection of the city impossible, opposition which Frederick ignored.

The Sulṭān's willingness to do a deal was due partly to his need to prevent Turkic advances, or as Roger of Wendover puts it, *the Sulṭān of Babylon was severely harassed by internal wars,*[1] but Frederick and al-Kāmil were in agreement concerning the futility of religious wars. Both regarded Jerusalem as no more than a political issue. To al-Kāmil, Jerusalem was just a sleepy, if sacred, city but a useful buffer against other incursions when held by the *Franj*.[2] To save face they agreed that Frederick would advance towards Jerusalem in a warlike manner, while al-Kāmil spread the word of the approach of a fearsome army. Frederick would appear to take Jerusalem by force of arms, and the Muslims would appear to defend those areas of Islamic importance.

As Ibn Wāsil told al-Kāmil, *We have only conceded to them some churches and some ruined houses. The sacred precincts, the venerated rock and all the other sanctuaries to which we make our pilgrimages remain ours.*[3] Similarly, it is claimed Frederick told the emir Fakhr al-Dīn,[4] *I have no real ambition to hold Jerusalem nor anything else; I simply want to safeguard my reputation with the Christians.*[5]

Frederick was as much interested in Islām as he was in Christianity, perhaps more so. He was taken on a tour of Jerusalem, and on finding a Christian priest entering a mosque, Bible in hand, the

---

[1] Roger Wendover, Frederick II, *op. cit.* Not Babylon in Mesopotamia which had faded a couple of centuries before, but a fortress in the Nile Delta.

[2] *The Race for Paradise*, Paul M. Cobb, Oxford University Press, 2014.

[3] In his history, *Al-Ta'rīkh al-Sālihī*, from the Prophet to 1240.

[4] 1211–1250, who acted in negotiations with Frederick.

[5] 'Sultan al-Kamil, Emperor Frederick II and the Submission of Jerusalem,' Maher Abu-munshar, *International Journal of Social Science and Humanity*, September 2013.

emperor angrily told him, *If one of you dares step in here again without permission, I will pluck out his eyes.* On Frederick's first night in the city, the muezzins refrained from calling the faithful to prayer to avoid disturbing him but next morning he exclaimed, *If I spent this night in Jerusalem, it was above all to hear the muezzins' call.*[1]

Given his attitude to religion, it is perhaps not surprising that Frederick was excommunicated twice, not that this seemed to bother him. As the Sicilian medievalist, Luigi Mendola,[2] wrote,

> [his] *reaction to excommunication merits mention in any record of cavalier indifference or sheer chutzpah by a medieval monarch.*

It may seem unlikely that Frederick was an atheist, but much of what he said does give that impression. In his upbringing, he studied philosophy and was certainly more scientist than cleric. Even while he was negotiating with al-Kāmil, he continued to pose mathematical questions which the Sulṭān had his scholars answer. Frederick has been called a materialist, someone who takes the view that there is nothing but matter. For a materialist the concept of a soul is meaningless.

Other crusades

There were further crusades up to the ninth, perhaps the most devastating being the seventh (1248-1254), also attacking Egypt. Its leader, Louis IX of France, was defeated by Ayyubid forces. In the lead up to the crucial battle of al-Manṣūrah, the Templars captured the Muslim camp but Robert of Artois, leader of the Crusader vanguard, stupidly and fatally insisted on a follow-up charge into the town. Horses could not manoeuvre in the narrow streets. Almost none of the Templars survived. At the ensuing Battle of Fariskur, the

---

[1] Maalouf, *op. cit.*

[2] 'Was Frederick II an atheist?' *Best of Sicily Magazine*, 2012.

Muslims destroyed the rest of the Christian army, embarrassed by the number of prisoners.

> *Finding it impossible to guard them all, those that were too feeble to march were executed at once, and on every evening for a week three hundred were taken out and decapitated.*[1]

Ibn Wāṣil takes the Templars' military prowess as the standard by which to measure all others. He wrote of the Mamlūks, the elite Egyptian cavalry, that *they were Islām's Templars* and they *caused the Franj terrible losses and played a major part in the victory.*[2]

Ruad

A Mamlūk commander at the battle was the great Baibars[3] who, having risen to Sulṭān, took the Levantine coast in 1271, including the massive castle *Crac des Chevaliers*. A later Sulṭān, Al-Ashraf Khalil finally drove the *Franj* out of the Holy Land. The Templars remained ready to support another crusade, one never likely to happen, certainly not after 1302 when the Mamlūks took *Ruad*. This tiny, waterless island of just 49 acres (19.8 ha), was the site of the Templars' last hurrah. There they waited for the Mongol Ghâzân Kahn to join an offensive against the Mamlūks.

Ruad

---

[1] Runciman, *op. cit.*

[2] 'Ibn Wāṣil on Louis's defeat and captivity' in Jessalynn Bird, *op. cit.*

[3] al-Malik al-Ẓāhir Rukn al-Dīn Baibars al-Bunduqdārī.

In 1299 a Mongol army had driven the Mamlūks back to Egypt, but had been forced to retreat because of what Demurger calls the Mongols' weak point — *the difficulty of keeping such a vast army of horsemen mobilised, not because the men could not be kept, but because their mounts had to be fed.*[1]

Ghâzân planned to attack again in November 1300 so the Templars crossed to the mainland, waiting there for three weeks, but again Ghâzân failed to arrive, blaming the harsh winter. The Templars returned to their tiny, miserably uncomfortable island, hoping for another mobilisation, but when it occurred, there were no Templars to witness it. In 1302, a Mamlūk fleet arrived and the Templars were slaughtered.

Next

Of what benefit were the crusades? Some individuals returned from Jerusalem to a transformed life, free from sin and guilt. Others, Tyerman writes, *were and remained extremely violent. Thomas of Marle notoriously terrorised the Ile de France for years on either side of his march to Jerusalem; the pilgrim remained a psychopath.*[2]

For Knights Templar fighting in the Holy Land there was usually no return. The nature of their religious commitment and the roles they assumed placed them in mortal danger. It has been estimated that 90% died. Rule 63 included the words,

> *I will avenge the death of Jesus Christ by my death. For just as Jesus Christ gave his body for me, I am prepared in the same way. This is a suitable offering; a living sacrifice and very pleasing to God.*

The number of sins forgiven and of souls entering heaven who might have otherwise have been refused, are statistics not available in this

[1] *The Last Templar*, Alain Demurger, trnsl. Antonia Nevill, Profile Books, 2004.

[2] Tyerman, *God's War*, *op. cit.*

life and so opinions on the crusades depend on the place of religion in society which of course changes.

> *During the Middle Ages you could not find a Christian in Europe who did not believe that the crusades were an act of highest good [but today] your average man on the street in both New York and Cairo would agree that the crusades were an insidious, cynical, and unprovoked attack by religious zealots against a peaceful, prosperous, and sophisticated Muslim world.*[1]

It may be helpful to view the place of the Christian religion, in society and in thought, in three phases:

(1) A single church owns the truth and is rarely questioned. Heresies are put down with force. Any opposing religion must be wrong (and evil).

(2) Following the Reformation and the growth of Protestantism, it becomes impossible for the original church to prevent new ideas. It still holds that it alone owns the 'truth' but other churches offer different 'truths'.

(3) Reason, not faith, becomes the deciding criterion of 'truth'. Deism initially attempts to combine reason with faith but fails. Reason and faith became opposing concepts.

Theology asks about the nature of God. Philosophy asks whether the word *god* has any meaning.

---

[1] 'Crusade Myths,' Thomas Madden, *Catholic Dossier*, 2002.

Opinions on the crusades

Early views

A contemporary of the crusades claimed they were the greatest event

 since the Resurrection.[1] At the time, they were part of the undeniable religious truth from which any deviation or opposition would hinder the soul on its way to heaven or even prohibit its entry. It was thought that Muslims could not be converted to the true faith and that their extermination was the only possible route. The text of Urban II's sermon at Clermont is lost but versions of it, all different and none likely to be wholly accurate, bear out this opinion.[2]

In the Fulcher of Chartres version, Urban calls Muslims *a despised and base race, which worships demons,* and while you should shudder *at raising a violent hand against Christians; it is less wicked to brandish your sword against Saracens.* In a gory version not to be repeated here, Robert the Monk has Urban describing Muslims as *an accursed race, utterly alienated from God.* Balderic of Dol's Urban claims that Christian blood and flesh, *akin to the flesh of Christ, has been subjected to unspeakable degradation and servitude.* The 12th century *Chanson d'Antioche*[3] has Jesus approving the killing of Muslims.

---

[1] *The Debate on the Crusades*, Christopher Tyerman, Manchester Univ. Press, 2011.

[2] Taken from 'Medieval Sourcebook: Urban II,' *History Sourcebooks Project,* ed. Paul Halsall, Fordham University.

[3] Richard le Pèlerin, around 1190. Jeanne Paule Beaupoil, Marquise de Sainte-Aulaire ed. Didier et Cᵉ., 1862. My translation.

When our Lord heard this, he turned towards them.
'My friends,' he said, 'People not yet born
Will come with sharp swords to avenge me.
They will kill the faithless pagans,
Which my commandments have until now forbidden.
Holy Christianity will be revenged.
So my conquered land, my delivered country,
In a thousand years time will be baptised and lifted up.
The holy sepulchre will be found and adored.
Those who will follow me as I have commanded,
Will be my children. I will deliver them
To the celestial paradise which is their inheritance.
And you, today are crowned with me.

While the 11th century church referred to its opponents as infidels, pagans and enemies of God, Muslims described Christians as *polytheists*[1] (and often so describe them today). They referred to themselves as worshippers of the one true God, and as monotheists. At the Battle of Acre in 1189, it is reported that Saladin told his heralds to cry, *Forward the monotheist army!*[2]

15th and 16th century views

The voyages of explorers brought into question the rationality of wars between Christians and Muslims. Amerigo Vespucci, Christopher Columbus, John Cabot, Hernando Cortes, and Jacques Cartier revealed indigenous populations who were neither Christian

---

[1] Christology (the nature of Jesus) encapsulates the variations of Christian belief, some of which would properly be called polytheistic. The *Russellite* system, accepted by Jehovah's Witnesses, has the Father as the supreme god, and Christ a lesser god. While masonic Knights Templar are required to believe in the Trinity, one suspects that few could explain its meaning. *Mysteryism* might be a way out: the belief that we can never understand God or the Trinity and that it is impious to even try. The amusing *Extreme monotheism* holds that the three are names for the same person: *Jesus* the first name, *Holy Spirit* the middle and *God* the last — thus J. H. S. God?

[2] *The rare and excellent history of Saladin, Bahā' ad-Dīn, trnsl.* D.S. Richards, Ashgate Publishing, 2002.

nor Muslim, with no knowledge of either. In *Deism*,[1] I wrote of Edward, Lord Herbert of Cherbury (1583–1648) who argued that no one could sensibly believe that God would cast into hellfire millions of Chinese who knew nothing about a book written in an unknown language by an obscure sect in a tiny country four or five thousand miles away.

The Reformation

Martin Luther 1483-1546

Often dated to the publication of Luther's ninety-five theses, the Reformation opened the door to examination of previously unquestioned dogma and led to new forms of Christian belief. It thus jeopardised the idea of one ruling church, and cast doubt on earlier justifications of crusades. In 1683 Claude Fleury rejected their basis.[2]

Crusaders were not called upon by Heaven to carry out hostilities against the Musselmans. Palestine did not, of right, belong to the Christians in consequence of any gift of God ... There is no command in the Scriptures for Christians to build the walls of the holy city, and no promise of an earthly Canaan as the reward of virtue. It is mere equivocation to call Palestine the Lord's heritage, and the land promised to his people. These expressions belong to the Old Testament.

---

[1] *Deism at the time of the founders of the Premier Grand Lodge,* David West, Hamilton House, 2018.

[2] French priest, lawyer and historian, known for his *Catechisme Historique,* 1683. Quoted in *Remarks on Ecclesiastical History,* John Jortin, 1805.

The Catholic church distinguishes itself from Protestantism on the question of faith. It argues that Protestants wrongly take the Bible to be the sole arbiter of faith, holding the interpretation of its meaning to be the right of any believer. The Catholic church agrees that truth emanates from the Bible but only in conjunction with traditional practice and the decrees of both popes and doctrinal councils. Interpretation of scripture is reserved to the church alone.

The Catholic church took up arms against those it defined as heretics with the same force as it did against Islām. Two of the more violent expressions of this were the 13th century crusade against the Cathars[1] and the 15th century Waldensian[2] massacres. Such actions became less and less possible as Protestantism grew.

Reason

During the 18th century, contemporaneous with the formation of the first masonic Grand Lodge,[3] the rise of Rationalism questioned religion itself and denied the value of the crusades. Gibbon described them as *the grossest barbarism*.[4] Hume depicted them as *the most signal and most durable monument of human folly that has yet appeared in any age or nation*.[5] Voltaire wrote that France was peopled with new knights and lords who were *fond of a life of war and dissipation*. He objected strenuously to the Pope's seeming proposal that anyone should be granted *remission of all their sins,* and that the gates of heaven be opened to them, *only imposing on them the gratification of*

---

[1] *The Goat, the Devil and the Freemason,* David West, Hamilton House, 2013.

[2] Its founder preached the Gospel in translation from the Latin as a layman, both heretical in the eyes of the Roman church.

[3] Usually dated to 1717 although recent research holds 1723 to be more likely.

[4] *The History of the Decline and Fall of the Roman Empire,* Edward Gibbon, ed. David Womersly, Penguin Classics, 2000.

[5] *The History of England,* vol. 1, David Hume, 1778, reprint The Liberty Fund.

their passion for plunder.[1] Later, Charles Mills (1788-1826) also condemned the crusades, but with the Knights Templar in mind, he temporised.

> *We can follow with sympathy both the deluded fanatic, and the noble adventurer in arms, in their wanderings and marches through foreign regions, braving the most frightful dangers, patient in toil, invincible in military spirit. So visionary was the object, so apparently remote from selfish relations, that their fanaticism wears a character of generous virtue.*[2]

Sir Walter Scott

The romantic 15th century Smailholm Tower, near Kelso in Scotland, where Sir Walter Scott visited his grandfather.

The early 19th century may appear to have softened the criticism of the crusades with the popularity of the works of Sir Walter Scott

---

[1] *An Essay on Universal History: the manners and spirit of nations,* Voltaire, 1756, trnsl. Peter Constantine, reprint HardPress, 2018.

[2] Mills, *op.cit.*

(1771-1832). The masonic Knights Templar may owe much to his chivalric romances. A freemason himself, Scott was writing when the ritual was forming.[1] His best known work, *Ivanhoe*, released in 1819, *turned men's minds in the direction of the Middle Ages* as St John Newman put it.[2] His *Talisman*, set in the crusades and depicting a chivalrous Saladin, was published in 1825, and *Count Robert of Paris*, with a plot set in a Constantinople during the first crusade, in 1832. He expresses admiration for Templars and Hospitallers.

> *It was after the conquest of the Holy Land that the union between temporal and spiritual chivalry ... became perfect, by the institution of two celebrated military orders of monks, the Knights Templar and the Knights of St John of Jerusalem, who ... taking on themselves the monastic vows of celibacy, purity, and obedience, did not cease to remain soldiers, and directed their whole energy against the Saracens.*[3]

However, the chivalric code had limits for Scott. He warned that when taken too far it led to vice. While bravery was a necessary condition for being a perfect knight, deliberately seeking combat made it a vice. Neither was he entirely an enthusiast of the crusades which, he writes, *inculcated religion, not as a check on the horrors and cries of war, but as itself its most proper and legitimate cause.* Religion has often been a vehicle for evil, if not always its source - hence the masonic injunction *not to be an enthusiast* (fanatic).

The crusades' most famous modern era historian, Steven Runciman, was of the opinion that the *Holy War itself was nothing more than a long act of intolerance in the name of God, which is the sin against the Holy Ghost.*

---

[1] Lodge St David, No. 36. Its Scott Night Dinner is held on the first Thursday in March following a wreath laying at the Scott monument.

[2] *Apologia pro Vita Sua*, Longman, 1864. Cardinal John Henry Newman

[3] *Essays on Chivalry, Romance and the Drama*, 1870; reprint Forgotten Books, 2016.

Nevertheless Thomas Madden, like Mills, is of the opinion that the motivation of individual Crusaders was often genuine enough.[1]

Islamic views

It is worth pointing out that the land of Islām was far more extensive than Crusader Europe. It ran from Spain to India and from Kazakhstan to the Yemen. It was more wealthy, more urbanised and culturally more diverse.

> [Europe was] *an impoverished, one might even say developing, region on the margins of the world. It was inhabited by a fanatical, war-like people, adherents of a backward creed. Its economy offered little besides cheap markets and raw materials. It presented some wondrous architecture and outré customs … but little else.*[2]

Contemporary Arab writers spoke *not of the crusades but of Frankish wars or the Frankish invasions* and the schism between the Arab and the Western world dates from that time, *deeply felt by the Arabs, even today, as an act of rape.*[3] Mourad writes that

> *In the Muslim public imagination of today, the Crusaders are remembered as medieval Christian barbarians who assaulted the Muslim world and slaughtered tens of thousands of innocent people, seen as medieval ancestors of modern Western colonialists.*[4]

Despite the tales of over-enthusiastic preachers such as Balderic of Dol and Robert the Monk, Christians had lived fairly comfortably in Islamic lands. They were of no great concern to the Muslims who referred to them as *dhimmis*, literally *protected people*, given the right

---

[1] *The Crusades Controversy: Setting the Record Straight,* Thomas Madden, The Dynamic Catholic Institute, 2017.

[2] Cobb, *op. cit.*

[3] Maalouf, *op. cit.*

[4] Suleiman Mourad, *The Conversation,* July 9, 2018.

to their own religion and released from military service by paying a special tax known as *jizya*. Qu'ran 9:29 reads

> *Fight against those People of the Book who have no faith in God or the Day of Judgment, who do not consider unlawful what God and His Messenger have made unlawful, and who do not believe in the true religion, until they humbly pay tax with their own hands.*[1]

The sting here is in the last nine words. Humility and obedience was expected in return for tolerance. The phrase *People of the Book* refers to those who have Abraham in their history: Jews, Christians and Muslims. They shared an interest when relics, supposedly of Abraham, Isaac and Jacob, were discovered at Hebron in what is now the West Bank, south of Jerusalem.

Mosque Macpelah, the traditional burial place of Abraham, Isaac and Jacob at Hebron. Gelatin silver stereograph, 1914.

Invasions

Christian invasions of Islamic lands started long before the crusades, and few Muslim writers see a religious motivation in them. They put the Franks' behaviour down to *their bellicosity and greed, which they*

---

[1] Muhammad Sarwar version.

were said to naturally possess.[1] Arabs and Berbers had moved into (modern) Spain in 711 CE, driving out the Christian Visigoths, who had earlier replaced the (sort of Christian) Romans. At its peak al-Ándalus, Muslim Iberia, included all of the peninsula except for Asturias, a strip along the northern coast. What the West knows today as the *Reconquista* (re-conquest), was seen by Muslims as a series of invasions from 785 in Gerona to 1492 in Granada.[2] Since neither Spain nor Portugal had existed before, the *Reconquista* is often considered as just a foundation myth for both countries, the *re-* being inaccurate

Having taken it from Byzantium in 902, Sicily had been held by the Muslims for nearly 160 years, when a Norman army under the brothers Robert and Roger Guiscard invaded. They completed their occupation 31 years later in 1091. The Normans had never been much interested in religion, only in land, as their 1066 invasion of England showed.

Hate crime

A recent change concerning the crusades has been their adoption by the extreme right. The Crusader cross, *often accompanied by the Latin phrase 'Deus Vult'*[3] *is a symbol often spotted on white supremacist marches. Crusader memes, such as an image of a Knight Templar accompanied by the caption, 'I'll see your jihad and raise you one crusade,' are popular on hard-right talk-boards and Facebook pages.*[4]

The murderer of 40 Muslims in Christchurch, New Zealand 'justified' his action as *revenge against Islām for 1,300 years of war and devastation that it has brought upon the people of the West.* In Trumpian capitals he

---

[1] Cobb, *op. cit.*

[2] El Cid, Rodrigo Díaz de Vivar, (d.1099) made his fortune fighting for both sides.

[3] More correctly *Deus lo volt*, God wills it, chanted by the congregation when Urban II preached the first crusade.

[4] 'What the far right gets wrong about the crusades,' Dan Jones, *Time*, October 2019.

wrote: ASK YOURSELF, WHAT WOULD POPE URBAN DO? The Norwegian, Anders Behring Breivik, who murdered sixty-nine at a youth summer camp in 2011, identified himself as a member of what was almost certainly an imaginary group of Knights Templar. One danger of the internet is that it gives a voice to irrational, probably damaged individuals but, as As'ad Abu Khalil writes,

> The Arabs notice, and will continue to notice, the resemblance between current Western political rhetoric, vulgar hostility and hatred of Muslims, with the papal rhetoric of the crusades.[1]

The other story

Warfare did not take up the whole of crusading's 217 years. Five or six generations were born in that time, and some would not have experienced a crusade. With a gap between crusades of sometimes 50 years, more than twice the time between WWI and WWII, they were really occasional events in the life of the Levant.

Islamic writers record the battles, but they also write of commerce, and shared religious buildings, as well as political and military alliances. Trade in wartime has often been observed. Mariya Grinberg[2] instances WWI when enemies continued to trade with each other almost to the end. The Arab travelogue writer Ibn Jubayr wrote,

> Though the fires of discord burn between the two parties, Muslim and Christian, two armies of them may meet and dispose themselves in battle array, and yet Muslim and Christian travellers will come and go between them without interference.[3]

---

[1] *Aljazeera*, Dec. 2016.

[2] 'Wartime Commercial Policy and Trade between Enemies,' Mariya Grinberg, *International Security*, Summer 2021.

[3] *The travels of Ibn Jubayr*, R.J.C. Broadhurst & Robert Irwin, Bloomsbury, 2019.

Some old Levant hands took on Islamic ways, addressing Muslim friends as *brother*, speaking Arabic, studying Arab history and the hādiths of the Prophet.

> *There was as much pragmatism as jihad on the Frankish-Muslim frontiers, as much accommodation, grudging tolerance, alliance making, and even downright friendship as holy war.*[1]

Some settlers stayed on after the end, and their names remain in Lebanese families: *Dikiz* (de Guise), *Bardawil* (Baldwin) and *Salibi* (from *salib* meaning *cross*).[2]

People of the book

As Anna Sapir Abulafia writes, a case can be made that the three Abrahamic religions, *people of the book,* worship the same God.[3] There is a continuity, if not an identity, between the God of the Jews in the Old Testament, and that of the Christians in the New Testament, but it is not recognised by Muslims. Muhammad did protect Christians.

> *No one is allowed to plunder these Christians, or destroy or spoil any of their churches, or houses of worship, or take any of the things contained within these houses and bring it to the houses of Islam. And he who takes away anything therefrom, will be one who has corrupted the oath of God, and, in truth, disobeyed His Messenger.*[4]

But that does not mean he agreed with them. Qur'an 29:46 says that a believer should only argue with Christians over *that which is best,* implying that there are important differences.

---

[1] Cobb, *op. cit.*

[2] *The Arabs*, Tim Mackintosh-Smith, Yale University Press, 2019.

[3] 'The Abrahamic religions,' Anna Sapir Abulafia, *Discovering Sacred Texts*, British Library, 2019.

[4] *The Ashtiname of Muhammad*, trnsl. Anton. F. Haddad, Baha'i Library online.

Next

We now turn to the people that the Templars protected; first the pilgrims, the reason for the Templars' formation, and then the settlers, the westerners who chose to live in the Crusader states.

These are better than those who have just arrived from their homelands, but they are the exception. I came across one of them when I sent a friend on business to Antioch, which was governed by Todros ibn as-Saf, a friend of mine. One day [Todros] said to my friend: 'A Frankish friend has invited me to visit him; come with me so you can see how they live.' 'I went with him,' said my friend, 'and we came to the house of one of the old knights who came with the first expedition.'

This man had retired from the army, and was living on the income of the property he owned in Antioch. He had a fine table brought out, spread with a splendid selection of appetising food. He saw that I was not eating, and said, 'Please, eat what you like, for I don't eat Frankish food. I have Egyptian cooks and eat only what they serve. No pig's flesh ever comes into my house!'

Another day, as I was passing through the market, a Frankish woman advanced on me, addressing me in her barbaric language that I found incomprehensible. A crowd of Franks gathered round us and I gave myself up for lost, when this old knight appeared, saw me and came up. 'What do you want with this man?' 'This man,' she replied, 'killed my brother Urso.' This Urso was a knight from Apamea who was killed by a soldier from Hamāt. The old man scolded the woman. 'This man is a merchant, and he lives nowhere near where your brother was killed.' The crowd melted away. 'The fact that I ate at his table saved my life.'[1]

---

1 'Orientalised Franks', Usāmah ibn Munqidh in Francesco Gabrieli, *Arab Historians of the Crusades*, trnsl. E.J. Costello, Routledge, 1969.

Pilgrims & settlers

The distinction between the two is not exact. Most pilgrims intended to return home at the end of their pilgrimage and most settlers travelled to the Levant intent on staying there. After all, what better place for devout Christians to end their days? However some pilgrims stayed and some settlers returned.

Palestinian leopard

Clearly, any pilgrimage to a near-war zone is fraught with danger, but the pilgrims' hazards were not limited to military action. Robbery, shipwreck, disease and exhaustion were the main perils but lions, leopards, bears, and wolves added to them.

The Jordan Rift Valley was and is subject to earthquakes, the result of the African and Arabian tectonic plates moving in the same direction but at different speeds. During the crusades the area experienced fourteen major earthquakes and many minor ones.[1] The 1202 quake,

---

[1] 'Earthquakes in Israel and adjacent areas,' D.H.K. Amiran, E. Arieh, & T. Turcotte, *Israel Exploration Journal*, 1994.

one of the largest in written history, reportedly killed a million people with its tsunami. The 1261 quake caused islands near Tripoli to disappear beneath the sea. Superstition would have amplified such events.[1]

Attractions

Despite the dangers, many sites drew pilgrims. Nazareth, Jerusalem and Bethlehem were obvious attractions but others had appeal: Capernaum for the feeding of the five thousand; Magdala for the birthplace of Mary Magdalene; Mount Tabor for the site of the transfiguration; Jaffa for St Peter's raising of Tabitha; Lydda to see the tomb of St George; and Mount Quarantene for the temptation. Sæwulf, said to be a native of Worcester, wrote a guide to Jerusalem for pilgrims in 1102/3. Here are some extracts.

> *From the Temple of the Lord you go to the church of St. Anne, the mother of the Blessed Mary where she lived with her husband, and she was there delivered of her daughter Mary. Near it is the pool called in Hebrew Bethsaida, having five porticoes of which the Gospel speaks. A little above is the place where the woman was healed by our Lord, by touching the hem of his garment. From St. Anne we pass through the gate which leads to the Valley of Jehoshaphat, to the church of St. Mary in the same valley where she was honourably buried by the Apostles after her death. Here is the brook Cedron; here also is Gethsemane, where our Lord came with his disciples before the hour of his betrayal.*
>
> *There is the oratory where he dismissed Peter, James, and John, saying, 'Tarry ye here, and watch with me,' and going forward, he fell on his face and prayed, and came to his disciples, and found them sleeping. The places are still visible where the disciples slept.*

---

[1] Which continues today. In 2015 a California State Assembly member claimed the state's drought was God's punishment for legalising abortion. In 2020, a Northern Ireland councillor said the Covid pandemic was God's judgement for the legalisation of same-sex marriage.

Next we come to Aceldama, the field bought with the price of the Lord. We go up by a very steep path to the place whence our Lord ascended to heaven in the sight of his disciples. On the spot where the Apostles stood with his mother, wondering at his ascension, is an altar of St. Mary; there the two men in white garments stood by them, saying, 'Ye men of Galilee, why stand ye gazing into heaven?' About a stone's throw from that place is the spot where our Lord wrote the Lord's Prayer with his own fingers on marble.[1]

Travel

Many pilgrims travelled by ship to the Holy Land from Marseille or the Apulian ports of Italy. Saewulf says that he travelled home on one of three ships, all carrying pilgrims, and a 1233 legal document at Marseilles implies that 12,000 pilgrims a year shipped with the Templars and Hospitallers. The document permits both *to load and unload in the harbour of Marseille two each of their ships twice a year … each ship may take on board up to a maximum of 1,500 pilgrims;*[2] this despite other legislation at Marseilles which restricted the normal three-decked ship to 500 passengers.

Jaffa was the closest port to Jerusalem but it could not handle the traffic. Benjamin of Tudela, who spent five years in the Holy Land, refers to Acre as the main pilgrim port,[3] and Theodoric, a late twelfth-century pilgrim, claims to have seen 80 pilgrim ships in the harbour at Acre on the Wednesday of Easter week.

Our perception of pilgrimage today is probably affected by TV programmes about the Camino de Santiago. Companies offer *customised and flexible itineraries, comfortable private room & bathroom, luggage transfers, 24/7 support, airport transfers, breakfast & dinners …*

---

[1] 'The travels of Saewulf,' in *Early Travels in Palestine*, ed. Thomas Wright, 1848.

[2] 'Carriage of pilgrims from Marseille (3 October 1233),' in Barber & Bate, *op. cit.*

[3] *Latin Christian Pilgrimage in the Holy Land, 1187-1291*, Elizabeth J. Mylod, University of Leeds, 2013.

food & wine tours, excursions.[1] A day trip to Santiago de Compostela is usually a secular experience, perhaps a coach excursion from a cruise ship moored at Vigo, the swinging of the *Botafumeiro* the highlight.

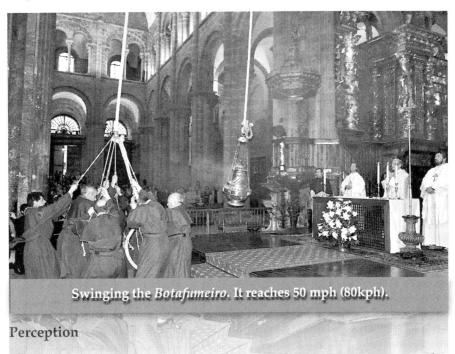

Swinging the *Botafumeiro*. It reaches 50 mph (80kph).

Perception

In the highly charged religious environment of medieval times, the experience would have been very different. Pilgrimages were made for release from sin. In the 13th and 14th centuries 500,000 pilgrims a year walked to Santiago de Compostela. The Russian Abbot Daniel journeyed to Jerusalem to witness the *Holy Light.*

> (A précis) *People from all countries come together on that day in countless numbers; the crowd fills the open space round the church and round the place of the Crucifixion. The crush is terrible in the dense crowd of people who stand, unlighted tapers in hand, waiting for the opening of the church doors. Then, the doors being opened, the people rush in, pushing and jostling each other.*

[1] Camino de Santiago Tours online. In 2019 there were some 350,000 visitors to Santiago. 41% were tourists.

At the eighth hour the orthodox priests with the clergy, monks, and hermits, commenced chanting the Vespers. During the reading of the first lesson, the bishop left the high altar, and looked through the grille, but seeing no light, returned. All the people, weeping, then cried out 'Kyrie Eleison' which means, 'Lord, have mercy upon us!'

At the end of the ninth hour the Holy Light suddenly illuminated the Holy Sepulchre, shining with an awe-aspiring and splendid brightness. Man can experience no joy like that which every Christian feels at the moment when he sees the Holy Light of God.[1]

Pilgrims passionately believed that what they saw was real and the relics they touched genuine. They had no doubts about the provenance of a sliver of wood from the true cross, a nail that had been driven into Christ's hand or the lance that had pierced his side, such as that found by Peter Bartholomew. At the time the papal legate called Peter a charlatan and Ibn al-Athīr refers to him *as a man of low cunning,* claiming that Peter buried the lance himself.

---

[1] Extracts from *The pilgrimage of the Russian Abbott Daniel in the Holy Land, 1106-1107 AD,* Colonel Sir Charles William Wilson, Palestine Pilgrims' Text Society, 1888.

On the fourth day he led them all to the spot with their soldiers and workmen, who dug everywhere and found it. Surprise! However, pilgrims believed what they wanted to believe. Carbon dating was obviously not available.

> *To eleventh-century Franks, familiar with the concept of saints, relics and miraculous intervention, Peter's experiences rang true. [With] a well-ordered system of belief in which the saintly dead acted as God's intercessors on Earth channelling His power through sacred relics, most were willing to accept [their] authenticity.[1]*

Relic of the chains of St Peter. San Pietro in Vincoli, Rome.

The night before Herod was to bring him to trial, Peter was sleeping between two soldiers, bound with two chains, and sentries stood guard at the entrance. Suddenly an angel of the Lord appeared and a light shone in the cell. He struck Peter on the side and woke him up. "Quick, get up!" he said, and the chains fell off Peter's wrists. (Acts 12: 6-7)

---

[1] Asbridge, *op. cit.*

Settlers

It is difficult to establish how many settlers there were in the Holy Land. One estimate is for 150,000 in a total population of two million, the settler population being about 7.5% of the whole.[1]

While most of those who participated in the people's crusade lost their lives, some survived and chose to stay, while others perhaps could not afford to get home. However, it is generally assumed that the first source of settler population was from the crusading armies and their baggage train. Many had taken their families along and many were tradespeople: blacksmiths, skinners, tanners, cobblers, tailors, millers, potters, vintners, butchers and bakers, able to work on the journey out as well as when they arrived. However, the indigenous people always remained the major part of the population.

Early on, the capture of a city was usually accompanied by the annihilation of its population, but fairly quickly it was recognised that a city needed people to function.[2] The Franks became more tolerant for the pragmatic reason that otherwise *there would have been no-one to farm the lands or to tax and the economy would simply have collapsed*.[3] Some Syrian Christians from *Outrejordain* (over the Jordan river) relocated to Jerusalem, although sixteen years after the capture of the city its leaders were still trying to persuade more to move.

Expansion was a matter of survival. Outremer states were too small to support the forces needed to defend themselves.[4] Towns competed

---

[1] That seems a lot, but Ronnie Ellenblum (*Frankish Rural Settlement in the Latin Kingdom of Jerusalem*, Cambridge Univ. Press, 1998) indicates that among the 1,200 villages in the 12th century kingdom of Jerusalem there were about 230 mixed villages, 19% of the total. If we assume a mixed village was 50% settler, the figure for settlers comes to 9.5% of total population. Not too far from the estimated 7.5% figure, especially given that the 50% settler ratio is just an assumption.

[2] Joshua Prawer, 'The settlement of the Latins in Jerusalem,' *Speculum*, Vol. 27, 1952.

[3] Jonathan Phillips, 'The Crusades,' *History Today*, 2015.

[4] Peter Eaves, *Crusader Castles in the Holy Land*, Museum of the Order of St John.

for settlers who came from many countries, attested perhaps by the *Rue des Alemans* and the *Spanish Street* in Jerusalem and by John of Würzberg's list of worshippers.

> For there are Greeks, Bulgarians, Latins, Germans, Hungarians, Scots, Navarrese, Bretons, English, Franks, Ruthenians, Bohemians, Georgians, Armenians, Jacobites, Syrians, Nestorians, Indians, Egyptians, Copts, Maronites.[1]

Promises

European population had soared during the High Middle Ages (1000-1250 CE) while agricultural output remained static. The combination meant pressure to find new lands. The crusader states offered a solution, but few Europeans had any idea of the Levant.

> The Holy Land existed as a virtual reality in the mentality of late eleventh-century western European Christians, a terrestrial relic, a metaphor for Heaven, a goal of life, the scene of the end of time and the Last Judgment as set out in the Book of Revelation.[2]

Settlers were attracted by release from sin. The Patriarch of Jerusalem invited potential settlers to *Come, come over here.*

> With the help of God we will undo the chains of all the sins of anyone who comes to our aid as long as he undertakes to do penance, and we will place him on the shoulders of the Lamb who removed the sins of the world.[3]

They were also attracted by promises of peace and prosperity. Symeon, Greek Patriarch of Antioch, invited them to hurry to *the land flowing with milk and honey and abounding in all good things. By the shedding of our blood all your ways lie open.*[4]

---

[1] Würzberg, *op. cit.*

[2] Tyerman, *Plan, op. cit.*

[3] *Ibid.*

[4] *Latin and Greek Monasticism in the Crusader States*, Bernard Hamilton & Andrew Jotischky, Cambridge University Press, 2020.

Gunter of Pairis enticed settlers with a fabrication.

The land to which you are headed is by far richer and more fertile than this land and it is easily possible that … you will acquire greater prosperity.[1]

Far from being *richer and more fertile*, the land was much more difficult to farm. Settlers introduced wine and pigs, but they could make little improvement on traditional farming methods. European deep ploughing would have resulted in the loss of soil through wind erosion, as in the 1930s American Dust Bowl.

Dust storm approaching Stratford, Texas.

Philosopher turned culinary researcher, Clifford Wright, is of the opinion that settlers could only *raise subsistence, not cash crops and although they were starting to learn more from the local Palestinian population, their mortality rate was so high that their continued existence was completely dependent on immigration from Europe.*[2] The only cash crops were the sugar cane and olives grown by the original

[1] Gunter of Pairis (in Alsace), *Hystoria Constantinopolitana*, ed. & trnsl. Alfred J. Andrea, University of Pennsylvania Press, 2021.

[2] *www.cliffordawright.com.*

inhabitants who continued to work the land, paying in cash and kind to their new masters. *Outremer* was never self-sufficient. Rather like today's seaside resort, it relied upon money from outside: from the military orders like the Templars, funded by their houses in Europe; from the religious houses, funded for the care of souls; and from the naval and merchant fleets on the coast.

Building

Castle building was vital to *Outremer* strategy, but while records show a large number of artisans and shopkeepers, there are few masons recorded. Runciman, in describing the Crusaders' siege of Antioch mentions, almost in passing, that when it was proposed to build a tower on the north bank, the project was held up by a lack of materials and masons.[1]

To put this into context, by 1330 when work ceased on the still incomplete Beaumaris Castle,[2] it had already cost £14,500, and wages alone were running at £270 a week. When challenged, Master James St George, one of the greatest architects of the time, replied:

> We would have you know that we have needed – and shall continue to need – 400 masons, both cutters and layers, together with 2,000 less skilled workmen, 100 carts, 60 wagons and 30 boats bringing stone and coal; 200 quarrymen; 30 smiths; and carpenters for putting in the joists and floor boards and other necessary jobs.[3]

The building had already used some 2,500 tons of high quality coal (burning lime to create mortar), 16,200 free-stones, 32,500 tons of other stone, 640 quarters of charcoal, 42 mason's axes, 8 loads of lead; 160 pounds of tin, and over 100,000 assorted nails. Agreed, Beaumaris is big but so were many of the Levant castles.

---

[1] Runciman, *op. cit.*

[2] On Anglesey (Ynys Môn) in North Wales.

[3] Tom McNeill, *English Heritage Book of Castles*, English Heritage, 1992.

Four hundred religious buildings were built or re-purposed during the 12th and 13th centuries, and further demand came from the planned villages revealed by archeology.

In the centre or on a hill above it, stood the manor house, sometimes incorporating a fortified tower. The church was located at one end or at its centre on the [one] street. The houses were small and narrow, constructed with thick rubble and ashlar walls plastered inside.[1]

Basalt, a hard volcanic rock, was quarried from the surrounding ditch for the building of Belvoir castle, near the Sea of Galilee.

Limestone, sandstone and basalt were commonly available close to building sites,[2] but wood was a great problem, its shortage chronic in most Islamic countries. Mark Master Masons might like to note that timber was to be found only in the cedars of Mount Lebanon and the Aleppo pines near Beirut. Deforestation was not new. Evidence on international timber trade is seen on the Egyptian *Palermo* stone, which tells of importing cedar from Lebanon as early as 2600 BCE.[3]

[1] *Crusader Archeology*, Adrian J. Boas, Routledge, 1999.

[2] 'Architecture in the Latin East', Denys Pringle, in Riley-Smith History, *op.cit.*

[3] 'Wood', Peter Kuniholm, in *Oxford Encyclopedia of Archaeology in the Near East*, ed. Eric M. Meyers, Oxford University Press, 1997.

Who were the builders? We know that the Templars had masons, but surely not enough to build 90 castles, 400 religious buildings, and all those villages. An account of the rebuilding of Saphet castle offers the answer of *operarii et sclavii,* workmen and slaves, but Richard McClary gives more detail in his analysis of Muslim buildings in Anatolia, during and following the crusade period.

> [While] *labourers were recruited locally, the stone masons were largely Anatolian, and probably predominantly Armenian and Georgian. It is likely that the majority of the higher-skilled individuals, especially those working with baked bricks and glazed tiles, were immigrants to Anatolia from Iran, and possibly even Central Asia.*[1]

This may imply a company, or even companies, of masons working for both sides, independent of the crusades.

Life in *Outremer*

Life for the settlers would have been as hard if not harder than in Europe, but at least women benefitted from the presence of Muslim doctors. Their knowledge and skill, far greater than that of Europeans, reduced the dangers of childbirth, the most common cause of female death. The difference between western and eastern medicine is graphically illustrated in this story.

> *The ruler of Munáitira wrote to my uncle asking him to send a doctor to treat some of his followers who were ill. My uncle sent a Christian Arab named Thabit. After only ten days he returned and I said, 'My! You cured them quickly!' This was his story:*
>
> *They took him to see a knight who had an abscess on his leg, and a woman with consumption. He applied a poultice to the leg, and the abscess opened and began to heal. He prescribed a cleansing diet for the*

---

[1] 'Craftsmen in Medieval Anatolia: Methods and Mobility', Richard McClary in *Architecture and Landscape in Medieval Anatolia, 1100-1500,* ed. Patricia Blessing, & Rachel Goshgarian, Edinburgh University Press, 2017.

woman. Then there appeared a Frankish doctor, who said: 'This man has no idea how to cure these people!' He turned to the knight and said: 'Which would you prefer, to live with one leg or to die with two?' When the knight replied that he would prefer to live with one leg, he sent for a strong man and a sharp axe. They arrived, and Thabit stood by to watch. The doctor supported the leg on a block of wood, and said to the man: 'Strike a mighty blow, and cut cleanly!' And there, before Thabit's eyes, the fellow struck the knight one blow, and then another, for the first had not finished the job. The marrow spurted out of the leg, and the patient died instantaneously.

Then the doctor examined the woman and said; 'She has a devil in her head who is in love with her. Cut her hair off!' This was done, and she went back to eating her usual Frankish food, garlic and mustard, which made her illness worse. 'The devil has got into her brain,' pronounced the doctor. He took a razor and cut a cross on her head, and removed the brain so that the inside of the skull was laid bare. This he rubbed with salt; the woman died instantly. At this juncture Thabit asked whether they had any further need of him, and as they had none he came away, 'having learnt things about medical methods that I never knew before.'[1]

As ever, members of the upper classes found it easier.

The great frontier-fortresses were almost as comfortably appointed as town houses, grim and fierce though life might be outside the walls. They had baths, elegant chambers for the ladies of the household and sumptuous reception halls ... When a knight was not in armour he wore a silk burnous and usually a turban.

Ladies adopted eastern fashions, often an under-robe with a tunic or coat, sometimes embroidered with gold thread and jewels. The life of men was generally very shallow. *Outremer* leaders took ostentatious

---

[1] 'Frankish medicine,' Usāmah ibn Munqidh in Gabrieli, *op. cit.*

titles. Godfrey de Bouillon became *King of Jerusalem*; Bertrand, *Count of Tripoli* and Baldwin I, *Count of Edessa*. His successor, Baldwin II, was also *Prince of Galilee*. Bohemond (1057–1111) took the title *Prince of Antioch*.

> *Fear made them brutal and treacherous and uncertainty encouraged their love of frivolous gaiety. As their tenure weakened, their feats and tournaments grew more lavish.*[1]

Settler Christians and Muslims were horrified by the extravagance and the immorality they saw around them. The Templars were protected by their Rule from the temptations of this life. When not at military readiness, they were committed to the routine of their monastery, to their oaths on poverty, and the limitations on clothing. No doubt they also felt fear but they expected to die and to be lifted straight into heaven. The Rule forbade them to retreat or surrender without being ordered to do so.

The loss of territory

Life in *Outremer* became increasingly cramped as its territory was reduced by Islamic advance. Increasing costs and decreasing revenues meant that inland defence had to be left to the Templars and others whose estates in Europe continued to provide funds. In the mountains of Galilee, Safed castle which the Templars re-built around 1240 at huge expense, was intended to protect 260 villages. It was garrisoned by 50 knights, 30 sergeants, 50 turcopoles,[2] 300 crossbowmen, 820 labourers and 400 slaves.[3]

Oliver of Paderborn, in his inimitable fashion, writes that *the primary usefulness of this building is that the convent of the Templars has been removed from the sin and vice that fester in the city of Acre.*

---

[1] Runciman, *op. cit.*

[2] Archers and light cavalry, often recruited locally.

[3] Anon. Few of the garrison seem to be Templars as such.

As territory was lost, it was maritime trade that kept *Outremer* alive. Routes ran through Levantine ports to India and China one way, and to Western Mediterranean and Atlantic ports the other. Matthew Paris speaks of £50,000 a year passing through Acre in the 1240s,[1] with trade in high ticket items: spices, silk, glass, ginger, saffron, perfumes, wine, furs and slaves.

The Silk Road, commenced in 130 BCE, prospered until 1453 CE.[2] Of course, it wasn't really a road but a number of routes with various start and end points, but all tending in the same direction with the same purpose. There was even a sea Silk Road from China around the Indian sub-continent.

Next

We now look at the other side, the people from whom the pilgrims and settlers were protected.

---

[1] *Chronica Major*, Matthew Paris, ed. Henry Richards Luard, Cambridge University Press, 2012. For comparison, the royal income of (English) King Henry III in 1240 was something like £31,500.

[2] It has been suggested that better names would be the *Jade Road* or the *Tin Road*, since it carried more of these commodities than silk

Part two

The other side

1036 CE Qur'an from Mosul, gold on vellum.

The Arab empire

There were obviously people living in the Levant when the first crusade arrived and there were others who came along later. Some were friends, at least at first, and others, defending their homeland, became enemies. As heavily armed soldiers, Crusaders did not come in peace. We start with the Arabs, known as *Saracens*, a word later applied to all Muslims in the Levant.

It has been said that Arab history is in two parts: the 1,400 years before Muhammad (570-632 CE) and the 1,400 years after. United under the Prophet, Arab armies created an empire larger than that of Alexander the Great and much the same as Rome. By 750 CE, it extended from modern Spain to Uzbekistan. It even influenced the Anglo-Saxon kingdom of Mercia ruled by King Offa (died 796 CE). He issued a gold coin, imitating one minted by the Abbasid caliphate, bearing the words *OFFA REX* upside down between the Arabic مُحَمَّدٌ رَسُولُ اللّٰهِ. (Muhammad is the messenger of Allah.)

The questions *Who are the Germans?* and *Who are the French?* are today relatively straightforward, even if history's varying answers have been dangerously complex. The Germans are the citizens of Germany and the French, citizens of France, although Guadeloupe, Mayotte, and Saint-Pierre & Miquelon may cause surprise.[1] However, like the question *Who are the English?*, the question *Who are the Arabs?* cannot be answered this way. Neither Arabia nor England are political states. Arabia has never been one.

Seeking a distinguishing and uniting characteristic, Mackintosh-Smith points to the Arabic language, although the language of the Berbers,[2] usually thought of as Arabs, is linguistically distinct, being related to the language of the Tuareg. Often called the *blue people* for the colour of their clothing, the dye from which, it is said, stains their skin, the 2.5 million Tuareg are traditionally nomadic, the principal inhabitants of the Sahara.

Tuareg singer Othmane Bali

Nevertheless, in the history of the Middle East, the Arabic language has served to distinguish the Arabs from the other major players of the time: the Persians who spoke Farsi, the Seljuks who spoke a form

---

[1] All are part, not colonies, of France, thus also part of the EU, using the Euro.

[2] From north-west Africa, Arabic Al-Maġrib [the Maghreb].

71

of Turkic,[1] and the Byzantines who, despite their Roman self-identity, spoke Greek. It is argued that it was the Qur'an, the first book ever produced in Arabic, that brought Arab speakers together rather than their religion. It served more as a linguistic reference point, for Arabs did little proselytising despite their beliefs.

> *It is remarkable how little the fight against the unbelievers aimed to unite them in one true universal religion, and how much it was to do with raiding them and imposing taxes. The conquests were less a matter of hearts and minds than of pockets and purses.*[2]

Settler and Nomadic

Tim Mackintosh-Smith writes of the two *rationalities* in Arab culture: the settled village dweller and the nomadic bedouin, the latter being the romantic view of Arabism.[3] The identity of a settled people is connected to the place where they live, but for nomadic people a place is somewhere they pass through, their identity being a matter of kinship and ancestry. The two rationalities at least partly explain the early success of the Arab armies, travelling light with minimal baggage, and their decline when home and belongings became more important.

> *Arab unity was more like a suspension than a solution ... the constituents inter-mingled happily as long as the mixture was kept in motion, by raiding and conquest. But when the motion stopped and the mixture settled, the constituents began to separate out.*[4]

The suspension settled out as the Arabs started to focus on what they had gained, and what they might take from other Arabs. Tribalism

---

[1] Later adopting Farsi.

[2] Mackintosh-Smith, *op. cit.*

[3] Mackintosh-Smith writes *Today, proportions of nomadic to settled Arabs are probably less than 1:100; but the nomad's-eye view of history still skews the way that both Arabs themselves and others view the Arab past.*

[4] Mackintosh-Smith, op.cit.

never was, nor is, very far from the surface. As Mackintosh-Smith writes, *you sometimes wonder if you are reading history or current events.*

The caliphates

Despite *As-Salām* (the giver of peace) being one of the ninety-nine names of Allāh, and the Arabic greeting *as-salāmu ʿalaykum* (peace be with you), succession between and within caliphates was frequently belligerent.

The first, the **Rāshidun** (632-661), was based in Medina. Its four caliphs are known as the *rightly guided* ones, and three of the four were assassinated. The first, Abu Bakr, ruled for just two years and in his time faced the *Riddah*, the turning back or abandonment of the whole or parts of Islām. The *Riddah* ranged from the false prophets[1] who sought to compete with Islām, to those who had signed up to the Islamic project but simply had not grasped the political implications of the deal. They continued to pray in the Muslim manner but *as for paying taxes to his representatives on earth, they let the matter quietly drop.*[2]

The fourth and last of the Rāshidun caliphs, Ali, was the most significant to Islamic history. It may seem to the outsider that Sunnī and Shi'a agree on most of Islām, and disagree only on succession from the Prophet. While the majority Sunnī, 85-90% of Islām, take Abu Bakr as his successor, the minority Shi'a believe ʿAlī ibn Abī Ṭālib, known as Ali, to be the genuine one. He was the son-in-law of the Prophet, the husband of his daughter Fatima.

Elected caliph in 657 CE, his rule was largely taken up in armed dissension, culminating in the first *fitna* (civil war) between his

---

[1] Predicted by Muhammad. Musaylimah was the most successful. He had his own holy book. When it seemed that he would become a serious rival, Abu Bakr sent a force to capture him. He was killed at great cost in lives.

[2] Mackintosh-Smith, op. cit.

73

supporters and those of his predecessor 'Uthmān. Accused of corruption, 'Uthmān had been assassinated in 656, but not before amassing a great fortune. Six years after his election, Ali was himself assassinated, apparently while prostrated in prayer.

The Umayyad caliphate

The Umayyads ruled from Damascus. Their bureaucracy was modelled on Byzantium, and not seen as genuinely Islamic.

> *The mosaics of Damascus are glorious, and also symptomatic of the Umayyad relationship with Islām: it was to be celebrated publicly and fulsomely, for it had got them where they were, but, ultimately, its glory was superficial, a glittering veneer,*[1]

words reflecting the great modern poet 'Alī Aḥmad Sa'īd 'Isbar, better known by his pen name Adonis. He describes the Umayyads as *an Islamic layer with a pre-Islamic essence, all given a Byzantine imperial gloss.*[2]

The Umayyads had a keen interest in the arts, particularly poetry and architecture. They invented the minaret and their masons built with superbly jointed ashlars. Both the Dome of the Rock and the Dome of the Chain in Jerusalem are Umayyad. They are also known for their desert forts or palaces. The largest was Qasr al-Hayr al-Sharqi, covering an area of twelve square miles, (28 sq. kms) of

---

[1] Mackintosh-Smith, *op. cit.*

[2] Quoted in Mackintosh-Smith, *op. cit.*

Syrian desert. It was built in 729 CE by Hisham ibn 'Abd al-Malik, a caliph who loved luxury.

His palace was paved with marble, each stone bordered with gold. He liked to wear a red silk robe, perfumed with musk and ambergris.[1] His son al-Walid II, a great lover of the grape, was assassinated in 744 CE allegedly for using the Qur'an as a dartboard and for calling the Prophet a charlatan.

In that same year, three other caliphs tried their luck. One reigned for six months and died in office, and another abdicated after two months, suffering from a brain tumour. Marwan II, the last Umayyad, managed five and a bit years but was overthrown in 750 CE by the Abbasids. Three hundred members of the Umayyad family were assassinated. One survivor, 'Abd al-Raḥmān, escaped to al-Ándalus (modern Spain) and founded a caliphate which became a centre for mathematics and science.

The Abbasid caliphate

Ruling from 750 to 1258, the Abbasids moved the capital to a new city built in 762 and named after the village at its centre, and made Baghdad the fabulous city of the *Thousand and One Nights*.

> *At the beginning of the ninth century ... the caliphate* [was] *the world's richest and most powerful state, its capital the centre of the planet's most advanced civilisation. It had 1000 physicians, an enormous free hospital, a regular postal service, several banks (some of which had branches as far afield as China), an excellent water supply system, a comprehensive sewage system and a paper mill.*[2]

In an Arabic golden age, cosmopolitan Baghdad was home to an amazing diversity of nationalities, outlooks, opinions and

---

[1] Mackintosh-Smith quoting Ḥammād al-Rāwiyah.

[2] Maalouf, *op. cit.* The West learned paper-making from the East.

philosophies. It was so cosmopolitan that only three of the Abbasid's thirty-seven caliphs had free-born Arab mothers. The rest were born from slaves or concubines from many parts of the empire. This made it all the easier for Turks to infiltrate the empire and use the Abbasid caliphs as figureheads. The people of the Prophet *lost control of their own destiny as early as the 9th century. Their leaders* thereafter *were practically all foreigners.*[1]

The famous Shabandar Café in Baghdad's al-Mutanabbi street, the haunt of poets, intellectuals, and book lovers. It was bombed in 2007.

Of the last two caliphates that concern us, the Shi'a **Fatimids** occupied Egypt, Judah and the North Africa coast. Originating in (modern) Tunisia, their name displays their supposed descent from Muhammad's daughter Fatima. The Turks drove them out of

---

[1] Maalouf, *op. cit.*

Jerusalem, but they took it back just in time to lose it to the first crusade. They were replaced by Saladin's Kurdish *Ayyubids*.

Warfare

The history of the Levant is one of almost constant, if often localised, warfare. The pre-Islamic archetype was the forty year War of al-Basus, which *foreshadows a disunity that has proven all but perennial in the Arab world*. It was fought between two related tribes, the Taghlib and the Bakr,

> *sparked off by an event that in itself was not exactly earth-shattering: what was shattered was a clutch of lark's eggs in an ... area of reserved grazing, monopolised by the Taghlib chief Kulayb.*

It was a camel belonging to the Bakrs which stepped on the eggs.

> *Taunts followed, but nothing more — until the suspected she-camel, waiting in line to be watered after the camels of Kulayb, broke loose and jumped the queue. Kulayb, incensed, took his bow and shot her in the udder.*

The women tore *off their headscarves, baring their heads to the battle and wielding their words: War! War! WAR!* and off it went, revenge causing revenge for the next forty years.[1]

Next

We turn now to Byzantium, the Orthodox Christian empire with its capital Constantinople and its inhabitants known as Byzantines. It was wealthy and powerful, renowned for its philosophical learning and artistic treasures. The early crusades to the Holy Land passed through its territory, needing its support, while the fourth crusade destroyed it. To understand this, we first have to see how it arose from the ashes of Rome.

---

[1] Mackintosh-Smith, *op. cit.*

Byzantium and the fall of Rome

By the third century CE the Roman Empire had extended over so many cultures that it proved impossible to manage. During the Imperial Crisis, from 235 to 284 CE, there were at least twenty-six emperors, four of them lasting less than a month, and the empire was on the point of collapse. A plague, probably smallpox or measles, caused severe manpower shortages. Revolts occurred almost weekly.

The tetrarchy

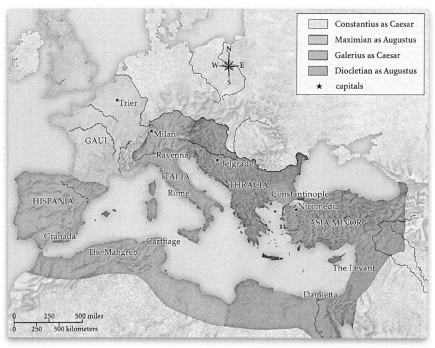

Diocletian, emperor 284-305 CE, took a grip and divided the empire into four, the so-called *Tetrarchy*, with two *Augusti*, himself and Maximian, each supported by a *Caesar*, Galerius and Constantius, as successors. Diocletian then took the remarkable step of retiring, persuading Maximian to do likewise. Galerius and Constantius took over, appointing successors themselves. However Constantius died while on manoeuvres in Britain and the army there proclaimed his son Constantine (the Great 272-337 CE) as their emperor. For a time there were six emperors. Thereafter, the traditional Roman method of succession, civil war, was re-adopted and Constantine came out on top.[1] He chose to rule not from Rome or even Italy, but from his new city of Constantinople. This eventually led to a division between the eastern and western empires and the rise of Byzantium.

The Huns

The decline of Rome had many causes, but invasions dealt the death blow. They were the result of movement westward, from 370 CE onwards, of tribes from beyond the Caspian Sea, driven by the Huns.[2] Under their famous leader Attila (395-453 CE), the Huns themselves invaded both eastern and western empires from 441. The final end of the western empire is usually taken to be 476 CE when Odoacer, a Roman general of Hun stock, deposed the last emperor in Italy. Procopius (c.500 – c.565 CE) wrote,

> *The renown of Roman arms had long since vanished, and the barbarians were coming into Italy in ever-increasing numbers …They continually seized more and more power, until finally they demanded a third of all the lands of Italy. When* [the Emperor's Regent] *Orestes refused to grant this they slew him. Then one of the imperial officers, Odovaker* (sic), *also a barbarian, promised to secure this for them if they would recognize him as ruler.*

He then dismissed the young emperor[3] and *gave the barbarians the third of the lands which they had demanded, thus binding them more closely to him, and ruled over Italy unopposed for ten years.*[4]

---

[1] Constantine is seen as the first Christian Roman emperor, although some doubt the sincerity of his belief.

[2] Possibly arising in northern China c. 200 BCE as the *Xiongnu*. (Zign-noo)

[3] Unusually sparing him, giving him a castle and an allowance for life.

[4] *The Gothic Wars of Procopius*, trnsl. H.B. Dewing, Loeb Classical Library, 1919.

It is said he had the imperial insignia sent to Constantinople because they were no longer needed in the West.

Visigoths

In the 4th century CE, the Goths separated into Visigoths (western or noble Goths) and the Ostrogoths (eastern Goths). The Visigoths visited a disastrous defeat on a Roman army in 378 CE, during which the emperor Valens was killed. The story is instructive.

Fleeing from the Huns in 376 CE, a tribe of Visigoths known as the *Tervingi*, sought permission to cross the Danube to gain the safety of the empire. The emperor Valens ordered that they be allowed to do so on the grounds that the empire had successfully integrated such people before and they *would provide a large number of recruits for the army, the numbers and quality of which were a constant source of imperial concern. Settled throughout the Empire, they would also bring land back into cultivation, and thus increase tax revenue.*[1]

However, a second Visigoth tribe, the *Greuthungi*, sought the same benefits, and while the Roman force was enough to disarm and admit one tribe, it could not manage both. Disorder led to the *Tervingi* being helped across the Danube largely still armed, while the *Greuthungi* found their own way across, fully armed. The Visigoths were then very badly treated.

> *The sea of tents and makeshift homes on the Roman side of the Danube belied the horrendous conditions they experienced that bleak, freezing winter. Poor sanitation and a crippling shortage of food made their life hell. In exchange for slaves and even children of some of the poorer Gothic citizens, the Roman generals gave the refugees fresh food. The Goths who had traded must have been doubly revolted to discover that they had bartered away their children for dog meat.*[2]

[1] *Barbarian Migrations & the Roman West*, Guy Halsall, Cambridge Univ. Press, 2007.

[2] *Ancient Rome: The Rise and Fall of an Empire*, Simon Baker, BBC Books, 2007.

The two Visigoth tribes then understandably ravaged the countryside in search of sustenance. In 378, the emperor Valens himself arrived with his eastern army and gave them battle near Adrianople[1] with disastrous results. The Romans lost between ten and twenty-thousand soldiers, the regiments suffering most being the elite, the least easily replaced.

The Visigoths next attacked Constantinople but were driven off with the assistance of a Saracen (Arab) contingent said to be *too barbaric for the barbarians*. As told by Ammianus Marcellinus, a soldier turned historian, a contingent of (probably) mercenary Arab warriors had arrived in support of Byzantium. They attacked the Visigoths who mounted a defence until one of the Saracens

> *long haired and naked, with the exception of a covering round his waist, shouting a hoarse and melancholy cry, drew his dagger and plunged into the middle of the Visigothic host, and after he had slain an enemy, put his lips to his throat, and sucked his blood.*[2]

The Visigoths surrendered to the Romans in 382 CE and seem to have been accepted into the empire in such large numbers that *whole units and even armies could be thought of as Gothic.*[3]

Things were now about to go very wrong for Rome, struck by invasion and famine while being ruled by youngsters: the western empire by a ten year old boy, and the eastern by one of seventeen.

> *Ironically … the female scions of the dynasty were strong willed and decisive figures, their male relatives were uniformly feeble, yet were the only family members permitted to rule.*[4]

---

[1] Now known as *Edirne* in the north-west of Turkey bordering on Greece.

[2] *The Roman History of Ammianus Marcellinus*, trnsl. George D. Yonge, G. Bell, 1911.

[3] Halsall, *op. cit.*

[4] *Ammianus Marcellinus*, John C. Rolfe, Loeb Classical Library, 1935.

Alaric

The Visigoths' leader from 395 to 410 CE was the famed Alaric.

> *No mindless, irrational thug, but a Christian and a man of his word. His troops were no hot-headed, marauding horde, but an organised and efficient army.*[1]

Entering Roman service around 392 CE, he was given a command of a Visigoth force, and took an official role enabling him to draw supplies for his men from the Roman commissariat. Turmoil in Italy meant he lost his title and more importantly his supplies, and so he marched on Rome. The senate tried to buy him off[2] with the title of *magister peditum* (master of infantry), a senior command, but what Alaric wanted, and indeed needed, was regular food for his troops. He demanded an annual payment of gold and grain plus land in northern Italy. Even when he reduced his demands, he received a negative response, and he besieged Rome again.

The Senate gave in but the emperor in Ravenna ordered legions from the eastern empire to seize the Goths.[3] Not a good idea. Alaric caught them in an ambush and, losing patience, sacked Rome in 410 CE.

Ostrogoths

Eighty years later Theodoric the Great led the Ostrogoths south to attack Constantinople. They were defeated by its walls and Zeno, the eastern Roman emperor, persuaded Theoderic to invade Odoacer's Italy to take an empire for himself. Theodoric obviously thought this was a good idea *and the whole tribe set out for Italy, taking along with*

---

[1] Halsall, *op. cit.*

[2] Halsall, *op. cit.* It had worked a couple of years before, when he had been given 5,000 pounds of gold, 30,000 pounds of silver, 4,000 silk tunics, 3,000 scarlet coloured skins and 3,000 pounds of pepper.

[3] Baker, *op. cit.*

them in wagons their women and children and all their movables.[1] In March 493, Theodoric forced Odoacer's surrender at Ravenna. The latter unwisely accepted an invitation to discuss terms at a banquet, where Theodoric personally cut him in half. Procopius gives Theodoric's subsequent reign a good review.

> *He dispensed justice with a strong hand, rigidly enforced the law and kept peace. The land was protected from the attacks of neighbouring barbarians* [and] *he allowed his subjects neither to suffer nor to commit wrongs; his own followers were given only the lands which* [Odoacer] *had taken for his supporters.* [Theodoric], *although bearing the title of tyrant, was in fact a righteous emperor.*[2]

Vandals

Another tribe pushed westward by the Huns, the Vandals crossed the Rhine into Gaul and went over the Pyrenees into today's Spain. With their own fleet, they sailed to North Africa. By 439 CE, they had conquered coastal Algeria and Tunisia including Carthage, the third largest city in the Roman empire. In 455 CE, following a dispute over a political marriage, the Vandals sacked Rome, hence the word *vandalism.*

Nearly 100 years later relations had altered and the Byzantine emperor Justinian sent 15,000 soldiers to assist the Vandal King Hilderic who had been overthrown. They were just able to defeat the rebels. The first battle teetered on its edge, but as the rebel general attempted to get his troops back into line of battle, Byzantium's mercenary cavalry attacked. *They were Huns, hideous, savage and implacable. The* [rebels] *took one look at the advancing horde and ran for their lives.*[3]

---

[1] Procopius, *op. cit.*

[2] Procopius, *op. cit.*

[3] *Byzantium, the early centuries*, John Julius Norwich, Guild Publishing, 1989.

A second battle three months later had a similar result, and the Huns then disappear from history. Perhaps because they acted so often as mercenaries, they became absorbed into other tribes.

View over Carthage, destroyed in 698 CE by an Arab army to ensure that Byzantium would not re-take it.

Next

The western Roman empire disintegrated, but the eastern part remained more or less shipshape. It became Byzantium, the Orthodox Christian stronghold. The word *Orthodox* in this context refers to those churches in communion with the Patriarchate of Constantinople, to be distinguished from Roman Catholic churches under the Holy See in the Vatican. There were and are doctrinal differences, particularly around the notion of infallibility, but that would take too long to expound here.

Byzantium and the crusades

Byzantium was left facing its traditional rival, the Persian empire.[1] The dividing line between them ran more or less north/south from the Black Sea to Sinai. Despite desultory warfare the frontier was never completely closed and trade continued - oddly enough including brides.

Defence

At the time of the first crusade in 1099, Byzantium ruled all of modern Turkey, Greece, Macedonia, Bulgaria and Serbia. The capital, Constantinople (now Istanbul), had impressive fortifications. Three sides of the city were bordered by the sea, and a heavy chain prevented unwelcome shipping entering the city's inlet, the Golden Horn. Only the north-west side needed attention and three lines of walls were built over the years, the outer in this image continuing the line of the 6th century bridge.

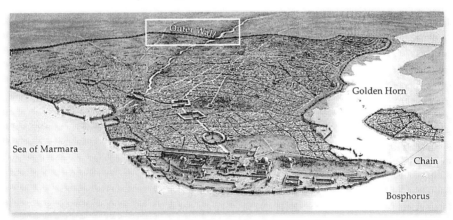

The Byzantine forces were highly effective, at least up to the 12th century. Its naval galleys were equipped with the much feared Greek fire, an early form of flame thrower whose burning liquid clung to its target and could not be extinguished by water.

---

[1] *Iran* was always the local name for the country. *Persia* was a Greek name.

This deadly concoction was created by a family of chemists and engineers from Constantinople, and the secret recipe died with them. John Haldon from Princeton University suspects [that] 'the key ingredients were a highly flammable light crude oil called naphtha and pine resin, which is sticky and would have made the mixture burn hotter and longer.'[1]

Its army featured infantry, archers, artillery and armoured cavalry. The stirrup, invented in China, may seem an innocuous object but it made possible the Byzantine *Kataphraktoi* [2] *(cataphract)*, armoured horsemen who advanced at a trot against an enemy softened up by archers. The lance, fastened to the horse fore and aft, put the weight of the animal into the point but by the time of the crusades they had become inferior to the faster and more manoeuvrable knights.

Earlier leather armoured Parthian cataphract showing the general idea. Byzantine cataphracts were more likely armoured with metal.

Their infantry was augmented by mercenaries, the most significant being the *Varangians* (probably Vikings), heavy infantry, famed for

---

[1] 'The napalm of Byzantium', Jamie Condliffe, *New Scientist*, Feb 2021.

[2] Meaning *armoured* or *completely enclosed*.

piracy and their itinerant life. Byzantine military developments included the *helepolis (city taker)*, an enclosed, moveable siege tower, and the bolt or dart firing *ballista*. Something like a giant crossbow on wheels, it was accurate over a range of 1,000 yards/metres.

Wealth

Estimates of the population of Constantinople at the time of the first crusade vary from 100,000 to half a million. Geoffrey Villehardouin[1] (*c*.1160-*c*.1213) estimated it at 400,000. For comparison, the populations of Venice and Milan, two of the largest western cities at the time, were about 35,000. London had around 15,000. When the leaders of the first crusade arrived at Constantinople they were given the guided tour and were astounded. They had seen nothing like it.[2]

Byzantium viewed itself as the centre of the world and its Greek speaking inhabitants continued to see themselves as Roman long after Rome itself was overcome. The 13th century emperor dined reclining on a couch as no one had done since antiquity, *watching, on the kalends of January,[3] a performance of dancing Goths, although no Goths had been in evidence for as long as anyone could remember*.[4] By dint of its geographic position, Constantinople was a trading and diplomatic powerhouse. Fabulously wealthy, it commanded the land route from Asia to Europe and the sea route from the Black Sea to the Mediterranean. With its engineering heritage from Rome, Byzantium built aqueducts, bridges, and harbours, and the 6th century Church of Hagia Sophia with the largest dome ever built until the 1547 Basilica of St Peter in the Vatican. From its beginning it had been a

---

[1] *Chronicle of the Fourth Crusade and the Conquest of Constantinople,* trnsl. Frank T. Marzials, J.M. Dent, 1908.

[2] *Oxford History of Byzantium,* (ed) Cyril Mango, Oxford University Press, 2002.

[3] In Imperial Rome, the first day of any month was known as the *kalends*. The *kalends* of January began the year, celebrated by vows of loyalty to the emperor.

[4] Mango, *op. cit.*

Christian state, even today its church seen as the spiritual leader of Eastern Orthodox, although less than 0.5% of the population are now Christian. While the western church insisted that the Bible remain in Latin, the Orthodox translated it to make converts in neighbouring Bulgaria, Serbia and Russia.

Hagia Sophia depicted by Swiss architect Gaspare Fossati.

Culture

Byzantium's most important legacy was the preservation of Greek knowledge and art. It linked *medieval scholars back to ancient Greek culture, and encouraged them to preserve texts by major philosophers, mathematicians, astronomers, geographers, historians and doctors by copying, editing and commenting on them.*[1] It possessed fabulous icons, early versions of both biblical testaments, editions of Virgil's *Aeneid* and Homer's *Iliad*, ancient medical treatises, gold and silver vessels, extraordinary glass *objets*, paintings, carvings, mosaics, and cloisonné

---

[1] Herrin, *op. cit.*

enamelling. Its wealth was its downfall. As Vyronis wrote of the fourth crusade (1202-1204),

> *Latin soldiery subjected the greatest city in Europe to an indescribable sack. For three days they murdered, raped, looted and destroyed on a scale which even the ancient Vandals and Goths would have found unbelievable.*[1]

Mosaic of Jesus Christ *Pantocratoros*
(ruler of the universe)

Next

In 1048, yet another tribe emigrated from the north (and east) of the Caspian Sea. The Seljuk Turks defeated Byzantium at the 1071 *Battle of Mantzikert,*[2] and advanced deep into Asia Minor. By 1091 they reached the Aegean coast, and established a sultanate in Nicaea, hitherto an important Byzantine possession. The Byzantine emperor sought help.

---

[1] *Byzantium and Europe,* Speros Vryonis, Harcourt, Brace, 1967.

[2] In the far east of modern Turkey. Listed by Paul K. Davis, as one of his *100 Decisive Battles,* Oxford University Press, 2001. He writes that this *defeat severely limited the power of the Byzantines by denying them control over Anatolia, the major recruiting ground for soldiers. The Byzantines were never again a serious military force.*

The Seljuk Turks

The emperor Alexios I Komnenos sought a small force, perhaps a couple of hundred knights, but Byzantium was

> *presided over by an emperor who was God's representative on earth. The empire was ... believed by many to form a central part of God's divine dispensation for mankind ... In Byzantium, some claimed, heaven and earth were one.*[1]

So the first crusade came about. Crossing the Bosphorus, it was the Seljuk Turks whom the crusaders first engaged.

Origin

The Seljuks emanated from those vast temperate grasslands, the Eurasian *Steppe,* which stretch 5,000 miles (8,000 kms) from Mongolia to Eastern Europe. Similar climactic regions occur in North America (the *Prairies* in the rain shadow of the Rockies) and in South America (the *Pampas* with the Andes to their west) and in the *Veld* in southern Africa. Alexander Borodin composed the symphonic poem *In the Steppes of Central Asia* in 1880. His notes to the score capture the feel.

> *In the silence of the monotonous steppes of Central Asia is heard the unfamiliar sound of a peaceful Russian song. From the distance we hear the approach of horses and camels and the bizarre and melancholy notes of an oriental melody. A caravan approaches, escorted by Russian soldiers, and continues safely on its way through the immense desert. It disappears slowly. The notes of the Russian and Asiatic melodies join in a common harmony, which dies away as the caravan disappears in the distance.*

---

[1] *Byzantium*, Peter Sarris, Oxford University Press, 2015.

Steppe grasslands in Mongolia

The Steppe was perfect for grazing but not for sustaining a large population. It was a population/food production imbalance that caused the emigration of Huns, Goths, Vandals, and Seljuks.

Empire

Adopting Islām around 985 CE, the Seljuks took religion seriously. Mackintosh-Smith argues that it was they who islamised the Levant, and not the Arabs. He raises the fascinating question of whether the Arabic and Aramaic speaking monophysite[1] Christians of the Levant saw these Muslim invaders as *slightly weird co-religionists*. Both practised prostration in prayer and they shared churches. When the Seljuks entered Persia, they espoused Persian culture and language, and their religious ardour and military skills led them to dominate the region. The caliph in Baghdad became their puppet.

---

[1] Monophysites believe in a Jesus with one single nature, divine, and were seen as heretics by an Orthodox Church which believed that he *came down from heaven and by the Holy Spirit was incarnate of the Virgin Mary, and became man,* as in the Nicene Creed.

Fortunately for the first crusade, the Seljuks were at first a loose agglomeration with their *atabegs*, military leaders, frequently at odds with one another. It was only during the reigns of Alp Arslān (1063-1072) and Malik-Shāh (1072-1092), that the Seljuks worked together to create an empire stretching from the Anatolian Peninsula to the Hindu Kush, the mountain range in Afghanistan.

Investiture of Malik-Shah I & his empire

However, as we have seen, civil war was the normal form of life at the time, so it is of no surprise that when Malik died his family quarrelled and the empire split. By 1096, the start of the first crusade, the Seljuks were once again engaged in fighting each other.

Misguided views

In 1922, the American historian William Stearns Davis (1877–1930) published *A Short History of the Near East*.[1] A child of his time, his work was no attempt at a disinterested and objective history. He made it plain that he had three strong principles: nationalism, democracy and Christianity. He measures history's societies against them which blinds him to the creativity of undemocratic, non-Christian, and certainly un-American cultures. His remark that stories of the *barbarous* Seljuks *are inevitably monotonous and bloody* is an example of this.

Seljuk achievements

Arab and Persian societies became highly skilled in what the modern Freemason calls *operative masonry*. The Seljuks were especially known for their *caravanserai*, built along their Silk Road to protect *caravans*, similar in concept to convoys. The buildings were substantial, fortified against bandits, many acting as military strongpoints. They were spaced at intervals of about twenty miles (30 kms), a day's journey for a camel.

It would have been rare for goods to be loaded at one end of the Silk Road to be delivered untouched at the other. More commonly, the load would be bought and sold at various stages along the route. To facilitate this, caravanserai provided overnight accommodation, baths, and prayer rooms, as well as the all-important bazaar. They

---

[1] Reprint Ulan Press, 2012.

became early forms of banks, using the cash-free system of *hawāla*, a word meaning *trust*. It is still in use.[1]

Sulṭān Han caravanserai, near Aksaray in Turkey.

There are two internationally known Seljuk intellectuals, one being Omar Khayyám. Edward FitzGerald's translation of his verses is entitled the *Rubáiyát* with its oft quoted stanza:

> *The moving finger writes; and having writ,*
> *Moves on: nor all thy piety nor wit,*
> *Shall lure it back to cancel half a line,*
> *Nor all thy tears wash out a word of it.*

Fitzgerald's title comes from the style of the poem's four line stanza. Khayyám uses an AABA rhyme, a *ruba'i*. For contrast, in *My Love is like a red, red rose,* our masonic brother Robert Burns uses the so-called *hymnal* stanza, rhyming ABCB.

---

[1] An explanation is available at Wikipedia under *Hawala*.

The name of the second intellectual is less well known, although what he created is famous enough. Jalāl ad-Dīn Mohammad Rūmī (1207–73), generally known as Rūmī, was an Islamic Sufi mystic. Sufism could be said to be to Islām what Kabbalah is to Judaism. Both go beyond the usual religious rules and commands, seeking a personal relationship with the divine. Rūmī's famous creation was a physical approach to meditation. He said *There are many roads which lead to God. I have chosen the one of dance and music.* Properly called *Sufi Turning*, its practitioners are often known as whirling dervishes. They seek an ecstatic trance through rotation, training to avoid vertigo.

Zengī and unity

The first attempt to reverse the disunity after the death of Malik-Shāh was made by the Seljuk Imād al-Dīn Zengī (1087-1146). Like Prince Hal,[1] after an unprepossessing start as a drunk, Zengī turned into the most dedicated of leaders.

---

[1] The young Henry V in Shakespeare's description of him. *Henry IV, Parts 1 & 2.*

His subjects and his army went in awe of him; under his government the strong dared not harm the weak. Before he came to power the absence of strong rulers to impose justice, and the presence of the Franks close at hand, had made the country a wilderness, but he made it flower again.[1]

For eighteen years he journeyed through Syria and Iraq, *sleeping on a straw mat to protect himself from the mud, fighting with some, sealing pacts with others, and intriguing against everyone.*[2] He maintained a web of spies and informers and his entourage contained no flatterers but only seasoned advisers. As with the Templars, discipline was strict. Ibn al-Athīr tells the story of an emir.

'Izz ad-Din ad-Dubaisi [who] *held the city of Daquqā as a fief from* [the Ata-beg Zengī], *billeted himself on a Jew. The Jew appealed to the Ata-beg, who sympathised with him. He had only to give ad-Dubaisi a look for him to pack his bags and move.*[3]

Zengī fell out with the Abbasid caliph al-Mustarshid Billāh and was defeated in battle in 1132. The importance of this event to our story is that Zengī's life was saved by a young officer named Ayyūb, the father of Yūsuf, better known as Saladin, who later used his father's name for his Ayyubid dynasty. This defeat makes Zengī's success in 1144, twelve years later, all the more surprising.

He scored a victory that rocked the powerful and humble alike, from Persia to the far-off country of the Almān and served as a prelude to a fresh invasion led by the greatest kings of the Franj.[4]

Zengī took Edessa. *It was said that even the birds dared not fly near, so absolute was the desolation made by the besiegers' weapons and so*

---

[1] Ibn al-Athīr, *op. cit.*

[2] Maalouf, *op. cit.*

[3] Ibn al-Athīr, *op. cit.*

[4] Maalouf, *op. cit. Almān* is Germany, French *Allemagne;* the *invasion* the 2nd crusade.

unwinking their vigilance. While his catapults battered at the walls, his sappers dug *into the bowels of the earth until their tunnels, propped up with beams ... reached under the towers of the city*. Set alight, the wooden beams fell and *the walls above the tunnels crumbled*.[1]

However, Zengī's old faults eventually caught up with him. In 1146, having hit the bottle, he was awakened by a eunuch slave taking a drink from his goblet. Idly promising to punish the slave next morning, he went back to sleep, and the eunuch killed him.

Nūr ad-Dīn

Zengī's second son, Nūr al-Dīn Maḥmūd Zengī (known as Nūr ad-Dīn) took over. *A just man who kept his word and was thoroughly devoted to the jihād against the enemies of Islām*, he also built a very effective propaganda machine.

> *Several hundred men of letters, religious figures for the most part, were entrusted with the mission of winning the active sympathy of the people and of thereby forcing the leaders of the Arab[2] world to flock to his banner.*

He had straightforward if not simple aims: to defeat all the enemies of Sunnī Islām, to reconquer the occupied territories and to liberate Jerusalem. He set out to create an Islamic force capable of taking on the *Franj*, although it was his lieutenant, Saladin, who gained the ultimate victory. He may not have slept on a straw mat, but he did avoid luxurious clothes and alcohol, the cause of his father's death.

He dispensed with his title Nūr al-Dīn meaning *light of religion*, and used his given name Mahmūd, praying, *O God, grant victory to Islām and not to Mahmūd. Who is this dog Mahmūd to merit victory?*[3] In 1146,

---

[1] *Ibid.*

[2] Malouf, *op. cit.* Perhaps he means *Islamic* here.

[3] *Ibid.*

told that the *Franj* had re-captured Edessa, he rode through the night and re-took the city as his father did before. Three years later, he destroyed a combined Crusader/Assassin army and took Antioch.

Saladin

An Armenian Kurd, Saladin was born in 1137 in Tikrit, a city in the centre of northern Iraq.[1] He died in Damascus in 1193, possibly of typhoid, at the age of 56 after thirty years at war.

> *A century and a half after his death, he would be remembered in Europe as the model of Saracen knighthood. England's Black Prince had Saladin's exploits embroidered on his bed-curtains.*[2]

He came to prominence in Egypt, having been posted there by Nūr ad-Dīn to resolve a dispute over the post of vizier in the Fatimid caliphate. Appointed vizier himself, he rose to power, dismissed the caliphate he served, founded the Ayyubid dynasty and was appointed Sulṭān of Egypt and Syria by the Abbasid caliph al-Mustadi.[3] He survived three attempts on his life by the Assassins[4] and was the most powerful Muslim leader for over 200 years, since perhaps al-Manṣūr, the founder of Baghdad.

The story of Saladin is really the story of the third crusade, and thus I have delayed describing it until this point. Building on the work of Zengī and Nūr ad-Dīn, it was Saladin who finally united *the political forces of western Asia in one purpose and imbuing them with something of his own tenacity and singleness of outlook.*[5]

---

[1] Near Ad-Dawr, the birth place of Ṣaddām Ḥusayn and where he was captured.

[2] Mackintosh-Smith, *op. cit.* The Black Prince was Edward, the eldest son of King Edward III. A model of chivalry, he commanded the cavalry at the Battle of Crécy.

[3] Caliph in Baghdad 1170-1180.

[4] Led for 30 years by the *Old Man of the Mountains*, Hassan-i Sabbāh, with fortresses in Persia and Syria. First known as *Asāsiyyūn*, (people of faith), or *Ḥashîshiyin* (hashish users), they assassinated at least three Crusader leaders.

[5] *The Life of Saladin*, Sir Hamilton Gibb, The Clarendon Press, 1973.

Gibb remarks on his ability to hold his army in the field when the typical Islamic army would have folded its tents and returned home. That is all the more impressive when one considers the polyglot nature of his forces, composed as they were of Turks, Kurds, Egyptian Mamlūks,[1] Seljuk mercenaries, Bedouins, and Türkmen, with contingents from Damascus, Aleppo, and Mosul. At the 1189 battle of Acre ships brought provisions from Egypt. The centre was commanded by Saladin himself with the Kurdish leader, 'Isa al-Hakkari, known as *Syrian Lightning*.

The lead up

Horns of Ḥaṭṭīn today, Galilee in background

At the all-important Battle of the Horns of Ḥaṭṭīn two years before Acre, Saladin's army of 30,000 had opposed a Crusader army of 20,000, the largest the Christians had ever put together, which had taken up defensive positions at La Saforie (near Nazareth). As bait to bring the Crusaders out, Saladin took a part of his army to attack Tiberias where the wife of Raymond III of Sicily was living. The bait

---

[1] So-called slave soldiers (see later).

was taken and the Christian force advanced on Tiberias. Saladin positioned his army between the available water and the Crusaders. Forced to camp overnight, thirst was multiplied by the heat and smoke, as next day the Muslims set fire to the grassland.

> *Night separated the two sides and the cavalry barred both roads. Islām passed the night face to face with unbelief, monotheism at war with trinitarianism, the way of righteousness looking down upon error, faith opposing polytheism. Meanwhile the several circles of Hell prepared themselves and the several ranks of Heaven congratulated themselves; Malik [the guardian of hell] waited and Ridwān [the guardian of paradise] rejoiced.*[1]

A Templar attack on the enveloping cordon failed through lack of support, and the battle ended as a comprehensive victory for Saladin and a tragedy for the Christians.

> *At the Sulṭān's command the King and a few of the most distinguished prisoners were sent to Damascus [for ransom] while the Templars and Hospitallers were rounded up to be killed … because they were the fiercest of all the Frankish warriors, and in this way he rid the Muslim people of them … A year later I crossed the battlefield, and saw the land all covered with their bones, which could be seen even from a distance, lying in heaps or scattered around.*[2]

Leavers and remainers

The decision to leave La Saforie was an example of how disunited the Crusaders had become. There was a strong view that they should remain where they were and let Saladin risk attacking a well-defended position. Those who wished to leave accused the remainers[3] of cowardice. A civil war does not help decision making,

---

[1] Imād ad-Dīn, 'The Sultan Saladin enters Frankish territory,' Gabrieli, *op. cit.*

[2] Imād ad-Dīn, 'The battle of Hittīn,' (*sic*) in Gabrieli, *op. cit.*

[3] Who turned out to be right, and not for the last time!

and the Crusaders had been close to it ever since the eight year old King of Jerusalem died two years before. The regent called a council at which Guy was elected King, but two members, Baldwin of Ibelin and Raymond of Tripoli, refused to accept the result. Baldwin joined the army at Antioch, while Raymond sought a deal with Saladin. When the Crusaders were surrounded at Ḥaṭṭīn, he led a cavalry charge and the Muslims opened ranks to let him through. Treachery or infantry tactic? Evidence for the former may be that having passed through enemy lines, he made no attempt to support his fellow Christians but rode on to his own safety. A Templar could be thrown out of the order for even talking about changing sides, let alone doing it (Rule 240).

From his victory Saladin went on to besiege Jerusalem which fell to him in less than two weeks. The Crusaders had attenuated their garrison to man the battle lines and there was little defence. They had also left much of *Outremer* defenceless, so that Saladin forced the surrender of Tiberias and Acre and took the ports of Sidon and Beirut within four weeks. A month later, he took Ascalon.[1]

Consequence

The disastrous defeat at Ḥaṭṭīn motivated the third crusade, led by the German emperor, Frederick Barbarossa, Richard I of England, and Philip II of France. Barbarossa was unaccountably drowned on the way,[2] so Philip and Richard became joint leaders. Early agreements seemed on the surface to preface cooperation.[3]

> *Philip promised to treat Richard as his friend and vassal, while Richard was to behave toward Philip as to his lord and friend.*

---

[1] Tyerman, God's war, *op. cit.*

[2] In the Göksu river which empties into the Mediterranean to the south of Turkey.

[3] 'The Third Crusade: Richard the Lionhearted and Philip Augustus', Sidney Painter in *A History of the Crusades*, Volume II, ed. Robert Lee Wolff & Harry W. Hazard, Univ. Wisconsin Press, 1969.

and there was history of them working together. They had joined to fight Henry II, King of England and Richard's father. Richard wanted Henry to declare him his heir and Philip wanted Henry to do homage as his vassal. The underlying reality was different. Richard had been betrothed by contract to Philip's half-sister Alys in 1169 when he was 12 and she 9, but he married Berengaria of Navarre.[1]

More significantly, Richard was head of the Angevin empire, ruling England, Ireland, and the western part of France from Normandy to the Pyrenees. Most of his adult life was spent in south-west France, and he spoke both French and Occitan, the language of the Languedoc. For his part, Philip fully intended to extend the lands of the French crown by ending the Angevin empire. In 1214, fifteen years after Richard's death, he achieved his aim at the battle of Bouvines, where he defeated an English/German army.

Acre

The siege of Acre, actually a double siege, was the most significant event during the third crusade. It had started when King Guy of Jerusalem was released from Saladin's prison in 1189. Surprisingly, given that his forces had been destroyed at Ḥaṭṭīn two years earlier, Guy managed to put together a new army of around 8,000 infantry with 600 knights, many of them Templars under Gérard de Ridefort, then Grand Master (and not the most impressive).

Guy launched a surprise attack on Acre's garrison which failed, and then set up a camp facing the city, awaiting reinforcements. Saladin marched on Acre to lift the siege but he also failed and arranged his army inland from Guy's. With the Crusaders unable to breach the walls of Acre and the Muslims unable to crack the defences set up by the Crusaders, stalemate ensued, as did famine and disease.

---

[1] There is little evidence that he had any interest in women.

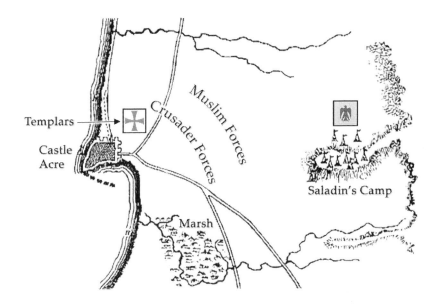

More than one hundred Crusaders were dying each day and desertion began. Some Crusaders went over to Saladin's camp, and others just wandered off to parts unknown.

Philip arrived on 20 April 1191 with six ships bringing more supplies and men. He built seven new trebuchets, iron screens to protect archers, and a Welsh Cat - a shelter, later armoured and wheeled, to protect sappers as they battered on or tunnelled under walls. With these new siege weapons, he launched more energetic attacks. However, in response to signals, Saladin attacked each time Philip did, giving the defenders time to repair any breaches.

Richard arrived just over a month later but was unwilling to respond to Philip's call for a combined attack. This has been interpreted as a power play and it is true that Richard finally wrested the leadership from Philip, mainly by throwing money about. Not waiting for Richard, Philip ordered more attacks but the defenders burnt many of Philip's siege engines with Greek fire.

As June 1191 moved on, a veritable avalanche of stones was rained down on Acre's defences, as Philip ordered the trebuchets to fire day and night. Two of the largest, Bad Neighbour (*Malam vicinam*) and God's Stonethrower (*Petrariam Dei*), the latter owned by the Hospitallers, blasted away at the Cursed Tower in the north-east corner of Acre's walls. All the other trebuchets[1] joined the attack, including one owned by the Templars.

At last a breach was made in the city's wall. To widen it, Richard offered one, two, three and finally four gold coins, easily a year's pay, to any man brave enough to run the gamut of the defenders' arrows and remove a stone from the breach. Enough did, the breach was opened and the defenders surrendered, at which point Philip returned home, no longer able to tolerate Richard's arrogance, it is said, but also because he felt he had done enough.[2]

Matters were more complicated than this account but it describes the main points. Successive interpretations and re-interpretations have vilified and praised both men in equal measure: the calculated, austere Philip for desertion and for achieving what he promised; the cantankerous, hot-headed Richard for humiliating Philip and for his later leadership. Stephen J. Spencer[3] analyses the many views on the third crusade and argues that there was no outright winner at Acre. Perhaps it should be seen as a score draw.

Richard and Saladin

More importantly, Spencer makes the point that victory and defeat was about much more than Richard versus Saladin, a relationship which popular culture centres its gaze on. As well as other personalities and forces, there are many factors to consider, such as health. Poor hygiene, overcrowding, insufficient food, and close contact with animals are all causes of disease and all were present

---

[1] Contemporary al'Nuwayrī says that 92 siege engines were used on both sides.

[2] Hosler, *op. cit.*

[3] 'The Third Crusade in historiographical perspective', *History Compass*, July 2021.

during the crusades. Dysentery, scurvy, malaria, leprosy (which killed King Baldwin IV of Jerusalem) and plague, laid soldiers and generals low. Saladin, Philip and Richard all fell ill.

Nevertheless, in popular culture Saladin is best known for his relationship with *Le Coeur de Lion* although the two never met. When Richard sought a meeting, Saladin replied that kings should not meet until an agreement has been reached. He was not averse to sensible proposals. In 1180, before Richard arrived in the Levant and with Syria suffering a severe drought, Saladin agreed a truce with the Christians which lasted two years.

This truce was unfortunately broken twice by the unpleasant Reynard de Chatillon, who first attacked a caravan of Arab merchants crossing the Syrian desert on their way to Mecca, and then ambushed travellers on their way to Jeddah across the Red Sea. A repeat offender, Reynard did time in an Aleppo prison for stealing from peasants, and Saladin had sworn to kill him. To the Muslims, he was known as Arnāt and it was under that name that he and Guy of Lusignan, King of Jerusalem, were listed among the prisoners taken at Ḥaṭṭīn.

> *Saladin went to his tent and sent for the King of the Franks and Prince Arnāt of Karak. He had the King seated beside him and as he was half-dead with thirst gave him iced water to drink. The King drank, and handed the rest to the Prince, who also drank. Saladin said: 'This godless man did not have my permission to drink, and will not save his life that way.' He turned on the Prince, casting his crimes in his teeth and enumerating his sins. Then he rose and with his own hand cut off the man's head.*[1]

---

[1] Bahā' ad-Dīn 'Saladin's character: his unfailing goodness,' Gabrieli, *op. cit.* Had Arnāt received hospitality, honour would have forbidden Saladin harming him.

Negotiations

Unable to meet the Sulṭān himself, Richard negotiated with Saladin's brother, al-Malik al-ʿĀdil, with whom he developed a sort of friendship, even with the occasional outrageous demand. At one time, Richard demanded feed for his hunting birds and at another, fruit with snow,[1] which could only be obtained by fast courier from the Lebanese mountains. Bahāʾ ad-Dīn reports a fanciful proposal.

> *al-Malik al-ʿĀdil sent for me ... and showed [me] the proposals that had been sent to the King of England by his messenger. He said that the plan was that he himself should marry the King's sister, whom Richard had brought along with him from Sicily.*[2]

The fancy was that the married couple would rule Palestine, and Richard would call off the crusade. This extravagant idea probably stemmed from Saladin himself. He wanted to keep discussions going to avoid conflict, but also he wanted to avoid a peace agreement. Bahāʾ ad-Dīn quotes Saladin's rationale.

> *When we have made peace with them, there will be nothing to prevent their attacking us treacherously. If I should die the Muslims would no longer be able to muster an army like this and the Franj would have the upper hand.*[3]

Saladin's emirs and counsellors agreed that the *Franj* would not abide by treaties, and advised *make a truce with them which will enable them to disperse, leaving no one in Palestine capable of resisting us.* Neither Saladin nor Richard took the marriage idea seriously.

> *The King's final message said: 'The Christian people disapprove of my giving my sister in marriage without consulting the Pope, the head*

---

[1] Bahāʾ ad-Dīn in 'Peace negotiations and the treaty,' Gabrieli, *op. cit.*

[2] *Ibid.*

[3] *Ibid.*

and leader of Christianity. I have therefore sent a messenger who will be back in three months. If he authorises this wedding, so much the better, if not, I will give you the hand of one of my nieces, for whom I shall not need consent.'[1]

A somewhat unlikely tale but Philip's decision to return home did present Richard with a problem. He felt sure that Philip would sooner or later invade his Angevin lands. So, having persuaded Philip to leave a large part of the French army in the Levant under his command, he offered peace to Saladin.

Both sides are tired, both companies are exhausted. I have renounced Jerusalem and will now renounce Ascalon. Do not be misled by [your] mass of troops assembled from everywhere, for it is destined to disperse when winter comes. If we persist in our miserable conflict we shall destroy ourselves.[2]

Saladin was again unwell and now in financial difficulties, so the 1192 Treaty of Jaffa was signed. It meant that the Muslims retained Jerusalem but allowed Christian pilgrims to visit freely, while the Christians continued to hold a reduced area of the Levant, a strip of coastline from Tyre to Jaffa, plus Tripoli & Antioch.

Going home

Returning from the Holy Land, Richard was imprisoned first by Duke Leopold V of Austria and then by the Holy Roman Emperor Henry VI. Leopold had fallen out with Richard at Acre, blaming him for the removal of his flag when he pretentiously raised it alongside those of Philip and Richard. Henry was allied to Philip of France, who by this time was really furious with Richard. It took fourteen months for the ransom to be paid, and Richard reached England only in 1194. He was killed five years later, besieging the irrelevant castle

---

[1] *Ibid.*

[2] Imād al-Dīn, 'Peace negotiations and the treaty,' Gabrieli, *op. cit.*

of Châlus, where his entrails were buried. *The rest of his body was entombed further north, in Fontevraud Abbey, but his heart was embalmed and buried in the cathedral of Notre Dame in Rouen,* interred in a small lead box which was actually found during a 19th century excavation. When opened, it contained a greyish powder.[1]

Saladin's death

Saladin had died the year before Richard's release. In Dante's *Divine Comedy*, he appears as a virtuous pagan held in *limbo,* the first circle of hell, referred to as *the Soldan.*

> *At foot of a magnificent castle we arriv'd, seven times with lofty walls begirt, and round, defended by a pleasant stream. O'er this as o'er dry land we pass'd. Next through seven gates … we came into a mead with lively verdure fresh. There, among figures of Roman antiquity, Dante espies, sole apart retir'd, the Soldan fierce.*

Saladin certainly did not achieve what he apparently conceived as an ambition. Bahā' ad-Dīn tells the story.

> *It was deepest winter, the sea was very rough with waves like mountains as God says in the Qur'ān. I had little experience of the sea and it made a deep impression on me. In fact I thought that if anyone had said to me that, if I spent a whole day sailing on the sea, he would make me master of the whole world, I could not have done it. I thought that anyone who earned his living from the sea must be mad, and that those who hold that any evidence, given by men who have been on the sea, is invalid are correct in their judgment. All these thoughts were caused by the sight of the tempestuous sea.*

> *While I was standing thus, Saladin turned to me and said: 'I think that when God grants me victory over the rest of Palestine I shall divide my territories, make a will stating my wishes, then set sail on this sea for*

---

[1] 'Richard the Lionheart's mummified heart analysed', Rebecca Morelle, *BBC News,* 28 February 2013.

their far-off lands and pursue the Franks there, so as to free the earth of anyone who does not believe in God.'

Next

The Seljuk empire collapsed at the end of the 12th century and was replaced by Saladin's Ayyubid sultanate which held sway until the Mongols' arrival threatened. When the Mongols took Baghdad, the only force capable of resisting them were the Egyptian Mamlūks.

Mamlūk Slave soldiers

I will use a capitalised *Mamlūk* to refer to those slave soldiers who created the Mamlūk Sultanate, based in Egypt and ruling the Levant and the Ḥijāz.[1] I will use the lower case *mamlūk* to refer to slave soldiers who served elsewhere. Just like the Templars in the Crusader forces, the Mamlūks formed the cutting edge of the 12th century Muslim army. It was their dynasty that put an end to crusading in the Holy Land.

For modern minds, the idea of a slave being an outstanding soldier is difficult to grasp. Why, we might ask, would any slave risk his life for someone who owns him? What possible motivation would there be, when the training was hard, the campaigning dangerous, and the opportunities for escape many in the fog of war? The secret, if thus it be, lies in a motivation largely ignored by modern management, that of *esprit de corps*. Mamlūks felt members of a special band. Their status was far higher than that of a household slave and higher than most ordinary citizens. Many became literate and, while still categorised as slaves, had opportunities for advancement and a high standard of living. Many were really volunteers, and fathers would even seek enlistment for their sons.

In the 12th and 13th centuries, the typical Mamlūk was enslaved as a boy from Kipchak Turks in central Asia. His price was three times that of a military horse, and the best were bought by sultans. It has been said that their education, with religious, literary and military studies, was the equivalent of Sandhurst or West Point. Once they became adult they began training in *furūsiyya*: the use of the lance, sword and bow, all on horseback.

---

[1] The west coast of today's Saudi Arabia, including Mecca and Medina.

Counterweight trebuchets in the Château de Castelnaud collection.

Their main weapon was the recurved bow but their artillery was also famed for its enormous counterweight trebuchets, throwing Greek fire and huge boulders. Some were capable of throwing a 400lb (180kg) rock, others could throw a 26lb projectile 500 yards (450m).

The Mamlūk sultanate

All Ayyubid emirs and sultans had their mamlūk guard on whom they came to depend, and who gradually took on high positions in government as well as in the army. They became superior to their masters in administrative as well as military matters, and eventually overthrew them. The result in Egypt was the Mamlūk sultanate (1250-1517). Becoming the fourth Sulṭān in 1260, Baibars was the most effective of all the sultanate's leaders.

A Mamlūk himself, born a Kipchak Turk born north-east of the Black Sea, he was enslaved by Mongols in Bulgaria, and sold to the Sulṭān of Egypt at the age of twenty-four, rapidly reaching the top. He assassinated Quṭuz, his one competitor for leadership, not an unusual act at the time. He took Quṭuz's hand as if to kiss it and stuck a dagger into him. He went on to unify Islām, putting down any rebellious atabeg.

> [He] *organised state finances, and established a communications network throughout the empire ... rebuilt fortifications and encouraged recruitment of troops, while at the same time encouraging the technical development of siege weapons and military/ political intelligence.*[1]

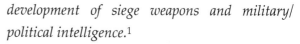

Only 15% of Baibars' army were actual Mamlūks. Like the Templars they were an elite contingent, although the Templars formed a smaller proportion of Crusader forces, perhaps 2% of the whole.

Baibars was much too formidable a general for the disorganised Franks. The Mamlūk campaigns were swift. Caesarea, Haifa, and Arsuf all fell in 1265. Antioch went in 1268, and by the mid 13th century, the Franks found themselves with no resources for offensive action. Even the strongpoints held by the Templars and the Hospitallers fell.

Fall of Acre

In 1271, Bohemond VI sought a truce which Baibars granted, since the Prince-no-longer of Antioch was little danger to him. As Ibn 'Abd az-Zāhir writes the 'Frankish king at Acre' sought a similar truce, sending *precious gifts of great value.* Baibars signed the truce and sent Muhyi al-Dīn, who tells the story, to the Frankish king for his signature. Seeking better terms, the King had his army line up.

---

[1] 'The road to Acre, 1265-1291' in Jessalynn Bird, *op. cit.*

'Tell him to observe whom we have standing behind him.' I looked, and saw that he had his army drawn up in full battle array.

'Say to him,' said the King to the interpreter, 'that he should look at this multitude.' I looked again, and bowed my head. He said again: 'Say to him: What do you think of what you have seen?'

'May I speak with impunity?'

'Yes.'

'Then tell the King,' I said, 'that in our Flag Store, which is a prison in the Sultān's realms in Cairo, there are more Frankish prisoners than all these.' [1]

Baibars died in 1277, and Acre, the last remaining foothold of the Crusaders, fell to the Mamlūks in 1291 under the eighth Sultān, ad-Dīn Khalīl. There are various accounts of the final defeat. Ludolph of Suchem, writing sixty years after the event, accuses the Muslims of promising safe passage for the defenders and then murdering them when they accepted. [2] The story is more complicated than this and composed of many small scale battles in the fog of war. At one point, the Templars disastrously charged the Muslim lines. The Hospitallers then attacked at night with no better result. Horses were of little use in the streets of the city.

A truce to allow the evacuation of civilians was on the point of being signed when a rock from a trebuchet landed near the Sultān. He responded with an all-out attack. The city was quickly taken, with only the Templar castle in Christian hands. The Templars with some locals were given free passage, but the Muslim soldiers managing the withdrawal started to round up women and children for slaves. The Templars killed them all. Eventually, the Muslims breached the castle walls and killed everyone inside.

---

[1] Ibn 'Abd Az-Zahir in 'Negotiations with Hugh III,' Gabrieli, *op. cit.*

[2] Ludolph of Suchem, *Description of the Holy Land and of the Way Thither*, trnsl Aubrey Stewart, Palestine Pilgrims' Text Society, 1895, reprint Brundage, *op. cit.*

The fall of Acre ended crusading in the Holy Land: 192 years after the first capture of Jerusalem and 92 years after the death of Richard. Abu'l-Fidā' commanding the Trebuchet *Victorious* wrote,

> *With these conquests, all the lands of the coasts were fully returned to the Muslims, a result undreamt of. Thus were the Franj, who had once nearly conquered Damascus, Egypt, and many other lands, expelled from all of Syria and the coastal zones. God grant that they never set foot there again.[1]*

The Mamlūk dynasty now controlled the Levant. Attempts to launch more crusades to the Holy Land after 1291 met with no success so that the ninth, 20 years earlier, no more than a series of raids, was the very last. Later crusades, if they can be called that, were really wars between European powers.

Codicil

There is a finale to the Mamlūk story. It follows Nelson's destruction of the French fleet at the *Battle of Aboukir Bay* in 1798. This left Napoleon stranded in Egypt where he had arrived as the initial step, so a theory goes, to attacking British commerce to and from India. Napoleon then proceeded to conquer Egypt, as much as anything because he had nothing better to do. He came up against the Mamlūks who had remained a force in Egypt. They were destroyed charging the French squares.

The only benefit of Napoleon's Egyptian escapade was the discovery of the Rosetta Stone, bearing a decree from Ptolemy V in three scripts - hieroglyphic, demotic (the people's script) and Greek - enabling the eventual reading of hieroglyphs.

---

[1] Quoted in Maalouf, *op. cit.* Abu'l-Fidā' was 18 at the time. He later wrote on history & geography and became an Ayyubid prince.

The Rosetta stone, now in the British Museum, always attracts visitors.

Next

On Friday 13th October 1307 CE, the French King Philip IV ordered the arrest of Jacques de Molay, the last Grand Master of the Knights Templar. In that same year, the vizier of the Mongol Il-Khanate finished the *Jāmiʿal-tawārīkh*, often referred to as the first world history. By then the Mongol empire covered 9 million square miles (23 million sq. kms). These events might have marked the passing of one era and the arrival of another, but then history often ignores poetic moments.

The Mongols

The Mongol conquest in the Levant reached its high water mark in 1260. They had destroyed Baghdad in 1258 and two years later took Aleppo and Damascus. However, their attempt to take Egypt in that year failed when a reduced Mongol army was defeated by the Mamlūks at the Battle of 'Ayn Jālūt.[1] Baibars played a leading role and when he became Sulṭān, he began the thirty year drive to remove the Crusaders from the Holy Land. The Templars made attempts to join forces with the Mongols against him. Understanding the Mongols will help understand why these attempts failed.

Chinggis Khan

Burkhan Khaldun

The first Great Khan was born near the sacred mountain Burkhan Khaldun in about 1160 and named Temüjin Borjigin. On his election in 1206, he was renamed Chinggis (probably meaning *fierce ruler*). A charismatic leader with political and administrative skills, he brought the region's squabbling tribes together,[2] naming the resulting

---

[1] The Mongol leader, Hülegü Khan, assigned the task of conquering the Levant, was forced to return to join the *Khuriltai* (literally gathering) to elect the next Great Khan. The Mamlūks defeated the detachment he left behind.

[2] Including the Tartars whose name was often used to refer to the whole.

collective *Mongols*. He ruled them as a conglomerate, not changing their ways but ensuring compliance to his laws. He offered the carrot with the stick. In return for obedience, he offered land, booty and slaves, land being the draw for nomads always concerned about pasture for their animals. Despite Chinggis's religious tolerance, introduction of a Mongol alphabet and a postal service, as well as enabling trade by ridding the roads of brigands, Runciman is severe.

> *He was completely ruthless. He had no regard for human life and no sympathy for human suffering. Millions of innocent townsfolk perished in the course of his wars; millions of innocent peasants saw their fields and orchards destroyed. His empire was founded on human misery.*[1]

Violence, as we have seen, was endemic at the time and the Mongols certainly were violent, even if Arab, Crusader and Mamlūk armies ran them close. Their violence was not necessarily gratuitous. It served to create a reputation and an expectation among potential enemies. Even the threat of it was a weapon, as seen in Ibn al-Athir's account of Mongol advances.[2]

> *Alas! I would have preferred my mother never to have given birth to me, or to have died without witnessing all these evils. If one day you are told that the earth has never known such calamity since God created Adam, do not hesitate to believe it, for such is the strict truth … No, probably not until the end of time will a catastrophe of such magnitude be seen again.*

Mongol warfare

The Mongol army was almost entirely cavalry. Women and men started riding in early childhood, and women took over the mounted

---

[1] Runciman, *op. cit.*

[2] *A Literary History of Persia*, Edward G. Browne, Cambridge University Press, 1902, reprint 2009.

work such as herding while the army was away. Every man from age fourteen to sixty was eligible for military service. Hunting ventures were used for training and both men and horses could operate in demanding conditions, survive on limited provisions and make long journeys across snowy wastes and dry deserts. They wore helmets and breastplates and were armed with lances, swords, and axes on occasion, but their main weapon was the composite recurved bow used by many armies before them. It was their numbers, speed and discipline that gave them superiority.

Mongolian riders in an historical re-enactment.

Conquest

The Mongols were nomadic, as many still are, and did not easily develop farming or artisan skills. They had to keep moving to satisfy a growing desire for manufactured goods and to provide pasture for their horses. Chinggis is said to have ordered all cities to be *razed so that the world may once again become a great steppe.* The historian Atâ-Malek Juvayni wrote,

They came, they sapped, they burnt, they slew, they plundered and they departed and with one stroke a world which billowed with fertility

was laid desolate, and the regions thereof became a desert, and the greater part of the living, dead.[1]

This is not altogether true. They often supported trade and commerce, trading raw materials like gold for silk, porcelain and glass. They press-ganged defeated soldiers, but they also welcomed volunteers, who were numerous. When seeking to take a city, they invested in gathering intelligence on the target's defences. They sent in envoys to hand its rulers *orders of submission*, demands that they accept Mongol rule. If their demands were met rulers would often be allowed to stay in place, albeit under *daruyačin*, civilian governors, and *tammačin*, soldiers to ensure the peace.

Ill treatment of their envoys was drastically punished. Indeed, any resistance was met with extreme violence and unconstrained brutality. Its apparent randomness increased fears. Runciman provides examples in his account of the activities of one division of the Mongol army in 1220/1221. What follows is a précis.

In the summer of 1220 the Mongol army entered modern Iran. They captured and pillaged Reiy, a city near modern Tehran, but spared most of the inhabitants. Next they took Qum and massacred its inhabitants. They did the same to Kasvib and Zenjan, but Hamadan submitted in time and escaped by paying an exorbitant ransom. The Emir bought off an attack on Tabriz, and the Mongols passed it by to attack Georgia. The Georgian army opposed them and was routed. Next they turned on the Kipchaks, who formed a protective alliance with other Caucasian tribes. The Mongols bribed the latter to stand aside as they crushed the Kipchaks, then murderously fell upon their erstwhile allies, who sought to bribe the Russians to aid them.

And so it goes on. The amazing effort did not seem to exhaust the Mongol force. A Russian army was destroyed in its turn and, after

---

[1] *Genghis Khan: World Conqueror*, trnsl. J.A. Boyle, Univ. of Washington Press, 1997.

some pillaging of a Genoese trading station and the destruction of a Bulgar army *en passant*, they re-joined the main body of the army.

Fragmentation

The Great Khanate had begun to fragment during the last years of the 13th century. Nevertheless Temür, the last Great Khan, still ruled 18% of the earth's dry land and 23% of its surface fresh water. He had been chosen in preference to his brother, Gammala, on the *Mastermind* basis that he could quote more of the sayings of Chinggis Khan. Unsurprisingly, then, on his death in 1307, the Mongol empire broke irrevocably into four.

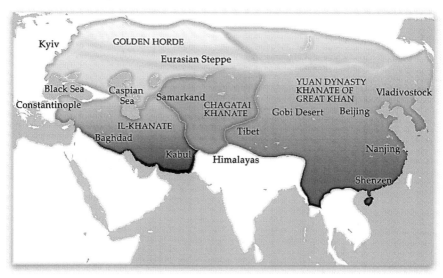

Nominally the senior, the **Yuan Dynasty,** established in 1271 with its capital in (modern day) Beijing, became more and more Chinese. It was overthrown by the Ming Dynasty in 1368. The most romantically named, the **Golden Horde**, not so called in its lifetime, stretched from the Urals to the Danube, lasting until 1480. Today the most memorable character in its story is not a Mongol, but the leader of the Kyivan Rus' who paid tribute to the Mongols. Alexander Nevsky is celebrated in Sergei Eisenstein's 1938 eponymous film with its score by Sergei Prokofiev. He defeated the Livonian Order, a branch of the Teutonic Knights, in the 1242 Battle on the Ice, which ended the crusades against Baltic pagans and Orthodox Christians. He was canonised when at his burial he raised a dead hand in absolution.

Initially a vassal of the Yuan Dynasty, the **Chagatai Khanate** split in the 1340s, lasting longest as Moghulistan, its eastern part (in today's Kyrgyzstan and Kazakhstan). Geographically closest to the Templars was the **Il-Khanate**, stretching from Asia Minor to Kabul, increasingly Persian/Iranian in nature. It lasted until 1335, long enough to change the Levant.

Contact and mis-communication

In 1246, Güyüg became Great Khan, leading to the first direct diplomatic contact between Mongols and Europeans. Pope Innocent IV had become so concerned about the threat that the Mongols represented that he sent envoys carrying two letters, now in the Vatican archives. One offered to save Güyüg's soul, and the other warned him against invading other countries.

> [Although] *the all-powerful Lord has so far permitted diverse nations to be laid low before you, He may not hesitate to punish wickedness in time and exact serious retribution in the future.*

Needless to say, this did not go down well. Güyüg replied at length, but the central message was, *Thou in person at the head of the kings, you must all of you come at once to do homage to us. If you do not accept our command, we shall regard you as enemies.*[1]

It is clear that neither party understood what the other was saying. When the Pope talked of *peace*, the Mongols thought he meant *subjection*. Words arrived with meanings at variance to those sent. Another part of Güyüg's reply demonstrates this.

---

[1] *The Mongols*, Morris Rossabi, Oxford University Press, 2012.

I have not understood this message of yours. You say we have conquered the lands of the Hungarians and others. Of course we have ... The Eternal God has ordered the whole world to be subordinate to the Mongols.[1]

When the Pope used the word *god*, he took it for granted that it would mean the same to the Mongols as it did to him. The Mongol word was *tngri* meaning gods (plural). Their beliefs were henotheistic, one god ruling over several lesser gods, with divine commands received through shamans. It was the top god Tenggeri who ordered the world to submit to the Mongols. As a mode of thought, the Mongols' explanation is really no different to Innocent IV's promise that *his* god would *exact serious retribution in the future* if the Mongols did not cease their advances. Culturally different gods giving culturally specific commands mark many conflicts, including Christian/Mongol and Christian/Islamic discords.

Witness

The Pope had entrusted his letters to two Franciscan friars, John of Pian and Benedict the Pole. The account[2] of their journey has been described as the first authentic description of the Mongols.[3] They witnessed the installation of the Great Khan, when a lot of mare's milk was drunk, probably fermented in the form of *airag*, 2% alcohol. John of Pian described the scene.[4]

Great quantities of presents were given him: silks, some with golden thread, stately canopies, silk girdles worked in gold, splendid furs that

---

[1] My edited version.

[2] *The Journey of Friar John of Pian de Carpine to the Court of Kuyuk Khan*, 1245-1247, trnsl. William Woodville Rockhill, in *The Journey of William of Rubruck*, 1900, Hakluyt Society, reprint Forgotten Books.

[3] Lance Jenott, *Silk Road Seattle*, Simpson Center for the Humanities at the University of Washington.

[4] Again, my edited version.

it was a marvel to see. He was presented with a kind of umbrella or awning to be carried over his head, covered with precious stones, and many camels with saddles, horses and mules covered with armour. On a hill there were more than five hundred carts, all full of gold and silver and silken gowns. On a high platform was the Emperor's throne of ebony, wonderfully sculptured with gold, and precious stones, and, if I remember rightly, pearls.

Alliance

When Möngke became Great Khan in 1251, he gave his brother, Hülegü, the responsibility of taking the Levant. The Golden Horde were enraged because they saw it as their patch, but when Hülegü destroyed the Assassins, conquered Syria, finished off the Ayyubid dynasty, and annihilated Baghdad, the Christian leaders were pleased. The Mongol attacks on Islām, and the fact that many wives of Mongol leaders had become Nestorian[1] Christians, raised hopes for a joint crusade but overtures received the usual Mongol response. Later, the reverse happened. The Il-khanate found facing the Golden Horde and the Mamlūks too much, and Öljeitü, Il-Khan 1304-1316, sought an alliance with the West, but was too late.

Europe had lost interest. Other matters occupied its collective mind. The Holy Roman Empire was involved with internal struggles and in rows with the Pope. The English King Edward I *(Longshanks)* was engaged in castle building to defend his Welsh dominion. His successor, Edward II, was bitterly resented by the barons, not helped by his defeat in 1314 by Robert the Bruce at Bannockburn. Crop failures caused the great famine of 1315 to 1317, killing perhaps 20% of the European population. Edward III effectively started the 100 years war in 1337 and the Black Death arrived in the Levant in 1347

---

[1] Yet more Christology. One way to describe Nestorian belief is that at the incarnation, the divine took over a previously born, pre-existing man. This obviously denies the immaculate conception and the divinity of Mary.

where it killed 30% of the population, and perhaps 100 million world-wide.[1] These events suppressed all and any appetite for Levantine adventures. In 1322, the Il-Khanate agreed an alliance with the Mamlūks, and then slowly disappeared, leaving behind only the fading Golden Horde.

Next

Step by step, the Templars also slipped into irrelevance as *Outremer* came to an end. It only remains to describe their final moments, to account for the lies told about them and the reason why they were singled out for interdiction.

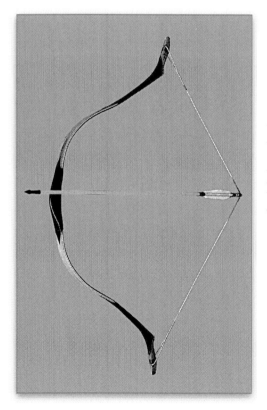

A recurved bow, the weapon that drove the armies of the Arabs, the Mamluks and the Mongols. This made by Csaba Grózer in Hungary.

---

[1] At the time of writing, Covid-19 has killed over 15 million. WHO May 2022.

Part three

Finale

The Last Templar
Friedrich Lessing, 1808-1880.

The end of crusading

In the last twelve years of Crusader presence in the Holy Land, instead of Christian energies being focused on the two great opposing armies, that of Islām and that of the Mongols, they were wasted in irrelevant squabbles about the legitimacy of Hugh III's right to the kingdoms of Cyprus and Jerusalem.

When his Aunt Maria's claim was rejected, she was allowed by Pope John XXI, who had an aversion to Hugh, to sell it to Charles of Anjou. War broke out in 1279. Charles was supported by the Templars and Venetians, and Hugh by the Hospitallers and Genoese. This folly was made worse by the Templars squaring up to the Hospitallers. They were supposed to be brothers-in-God. Templar Rule 168 said that if the piebald banner were to fall in battle, Templars must seek first to join the Hospitaller ensign, white cross on a red background.

Jerusalem

The first crusade had been the only one to capture Jerusalem by force of arms. The city had been held for eighty-eight years until Saladin retrieved it for Islām. Another forty-two years on, it was re-gained in the deal made by Frederick II but just fifteen years after that Khwarazmian mercenaries[1] re-took it in passing on their way south to fight for the Sulṭān of Egypt. They demolished the city such that it lost all importance, remaining a backwater until the Ottoman Suleiman the Magnificent (1520-1566) had a dream. He rebuilt the city's walls and created water gardens with beautiful fountains like those still seen today in the Alhambra at Granada (right).

There were other crusades but the raison d'être of the Templars and Hospitallers had been the recovery and retention of the Holy Land,

---

[1] The Khwarazmians ruled in central Asia from about 1077 to 1231, until they were forced out by the Mongols. Many Khwarazmians became mercenaries.

and it was for this that their funds were generated.The end of crusading in the Levant left the military orders at a loss. While the Templars dallied with the Mongols on Ruad, the Hospitallers had retreated to Cyprus. Their presence was unwelcome, so in 1306 they invaded Rhodes. Pushed out of there by the Ottomans in 1522, they moved to Malta, as every masonic Knight of Malta knows, for the rent of a falcon a year.

An aside

The 1941 film *The Maltese Falcon,* directed by John Huston, is based on Dashiell Hammett's great 1930 novel of the same name. In the film's trailer, Sydney Greenstreet speaks to the prospective audience.[1]

> *Come closer. I want to talk to you. I'm going to tell you an astounding story — the story of the Maltese Falcon. For six hundred years the Falcon has carried the mystery of fabulous wealth under its grotesque wings. I can tell you a thousand tales of the men and women who have*

[1] 'Chasing the Maltese Falcon: on the fabrications of a film prop,' Vivian Sobchack, *Journal of Visual Culture,* 2007.

hunted the evil bird. Every story has the same ending — murder.

As the film begins, a black falcon appears and over it, the words:

In 1539, the Knight Templars of Malta, [sic] paid tribute to Charles V of Spain, sending him a Golden Falcon encrusted from beak to claw with rarest jewels — but pirates seized the galley and the fate of the Maltese Falcon remains a mystery to this day.

Humphrey Bogart, Peter Lorre, Mary Astor & Sydney Greenstreet in *The Maltese Falcon*.

In the film itself, Kasper Gutman (Greenstreet) tells private eye Sam Spade (Bogart) of an elaborate tale in which a falcon disappears and re-appears across Europe over the centuries, eventually enamelled with black paint to disguise its value.

Dashiell Hammett said of the story, *All I can remember is that somewhere I had read of the peculiar rental agreement between Charles V and the Order of the Hospital of St. John of Jerusalem.*

Dissolution

The Templars were dissolved in 1312. Many theories have been offered in explanation, one cinematic version blaming the loss of the

Holy Grail[1] and an affair with the Queen of France, neither very likely. Other explanations and reasons include:

Old news

Alain Demurger sees them as redundant in a France where private armies no longer fitted as it became a centralised monarchy under the House of Capet, the ruling dynasty from 987 to 1328 CE. The Templars had become an embarrassment, yesterday's news.

Follow the Money

It is argued that King Philip IV of France destroyed the Templars' to get at their money. He was indeed financially embarrassed and his initial attempt to resolve his finances was decidedly unpopular. In 1295, he debased the currency, reducing the silver/gold content of new coins, re-paying loans made in the original with the debased coinage. The result was inflation and riots which ironically caused him to take refuge in the Paris Temple, the Templars' headquarters.[2]

Re-establishing the coinage required a large amount of bullion so Philip banned its movement out of the country, expelled the Jews while seizing their assets, taxed the clergy at 50% of income, arrested the Lombards who had made him loans and took half of everyone's silver. So, it is quite probable that Philip coveted the Templar's wealth.

Nevertheless, when the Order was destroyed Philip was forced by Clement V's 1312 bull *Ad providam* to give its assets to the Hospitallers,

> *who as athletes of the Lord expose themselves to the danger of death for the defence of the faith, bearing heavy losses in lands overseas.*

---

[1] A cup from which Jesus drank, a dish from which he ate, or even a magic stone.

[2] Barber, *op.cit.* The building was demolished in 1808.

Rationalisation

The defeat of the god or gods of any religion demands explanation and rationalisation for its believers. In 589 BCE, the Babylonian destruction of Jerusalem was rationalised as the Israelites' failure to keep their side of the covenant with YHWH, but to modern minds, the failure of the Templars in the Holy Land is less mystically explained. They faced an enemy based in its own land, with shorter supply lines, a constant and rapid source of reinforcements and, at a critical point, a unified army. Nevertheless, to the medieval mind the crusades were much more than a conflict between two armies.

> *God has ordained a tournament between Heaven and Hell, and sends to all his friends who wish to defend him, that they fail him not.*[1]

Hell had beaten heaven in the joust, and the Knights Templar, as Christ's champions, had let him down. Christ's defeat by Satan was rationalised as the result of the Templars' behaviour, so bad that God allowed the triumph of the pagans. Such rationalisation recurs in a letter from Pope Alexander IV.

> *No enemy opposition will harm those who do not allow themselves to be mastered by depravity of vices or dissension among themselves.*[2]

Repeated failure

Failures reduced the funding of further crusades and had a deleterious effect on the motivation of the soldiers. While Pope Alexander IV blamed the Crusaders for letting God down, Ricaut Bonomel's poem *La colère et la douleur d'un templier en Terre Sainte*[3] claims God was letting the Crusaders down. Anyone must be mad,

---

[1] *The Making of the Middle Ages*, Richard William Southern, Pimlico, 1993.

[2] 'Clamat in Auribus, 1261' (Listen to the cries) in *Jessalyn Bird et al.*

[3] 'The anger and the sorrow of a Templar in the Holy Land', Ricaut Bonomel (1265), in Barber & Bate, *op. cit.* My translation.

Who takes the fight against the Turks,

Because Jesus Christ does not oppose them at all,

For they have conquered and continue to conquer, to our great pain.

Franks and Tartars, Armenians and Persians,

Every day they are victorious over us,

For God sleeps, when he used to be vigilant,

And Mahomet acts with all his might,

To enable Melicadefer[1] to do the same.

Jaye Puckett suggests:

The tone of the songs surrounding the later crusades (fifth through eighth) is considerably darker ... optimism is replaced by doubt, cajolement by threats.[2]

Once the crusade had become a matter of furthering the political interests of one group of Christians by the slaughter of another, the troubadours could not continue writing as before.[3] Nevertheless, religious, military and public opinion continued to hold that victory over Islām was inevitable and that taking the cross was God's test to identify those who were worthy. Anyone truly fighting for God would unquestionably prevail and thus, by definition, anyone who did not prevail, must be unworthy (an *indefeasible proposition*).

Rumours

A rich and successful organisation like the Templars was bound to attract negative publicity. I have written elsewhere of the 'standard' list of accusations against *people we really don't like*, a list which includes secretly performing witchcraft, rape, incest, fomenting rebellion, and child murder with optional extras such as causing

---

[1] Puckett glosses this as *Malik-Adh Dhaher*, 'the illustrious king', meaning Baibars.

[2] Jaye Puckett, *'Reconmenciez novele estoire: The Troubadours and the Rhetoric of the Later Crusades'*, MLN, 2001.

[3] *Ibid.*

volcanic eruptions, floods, pestilence and famine. Even Jesus was accused of being a devil worshipper:

> Then they brought him a demon-possessed man who was blind and mute, and Jesus healed him … But when the Pharisees heard this, they said, 'It is only by Beelzebul (sic), the prince of demons, that this fellow drives out demons.'[1]

So there are several reasons proposed for the end of the Templars.

- They were an embarrassment, yesterday's news.
- The King of France wanted their money.
- Christ's defeat by Satan needed rationalisation.
- There was disenchantment with repeated failure
- Rumours were spread of indecent behaviour.

Next

While these reasons played a part, they are insufficient to explain the dissolution. They all ignore the fact that the Templars were a creature of the Pope. The real story of their end is more complex.

---

[1] West, *Goat, op.cit.*

Politics and torture

In what follows, it should be kept in mind that the Templars belonged to the Pope. In 1139, just ten years after the Council of Troyes during which the Templars received papal blessing, Innocent II issued the bull *Omne Datum Optimum*,[1] declaring,

> *We establish that the house or the Temple in which you are gathered ... shall be under the guardianship and protection of the Apostolic See for all time to come.*

and

> *If anyone, with the knowledge of this our decree, rashly attempts to act against it ... he will find himself accused of perpetrated injustice before the divine court and be unworthy of the most holy body and blood of our God, Lord and Saviour Jesus Christ, and also be subject to severe vengeance at the final judgment.*

The Templars had their own chaplain brothers with complete responsibility for their religious life. Rule 269 reads,

> *The chaplain brothers should hear the confessions of the brothers; no brother should make confession to anyone but him ... for they have greater power to absolve them on behalf of the Pope than an archbishop.*

It could not be a lot clearer. The Pope had complete jurisdiction over the Templars and the steps Philip IV of France took in 1307 were illegal - and worse - not that he was bothered.

Insinuation

Pope Clement V's 1312 bull *Vox in excelso* seems a very strange document, given Innocent II's declaration that the Templars would *be under the guardianship and protection of the Apostolic See for all time to*

---

[1] *Every perfect gift*, from Epistle of James 1:17. *Every good gift and every perfect gift is from above, and cometh down from the Father of lights, with whom is no variableness, neither shadow of turning.*

come. He offered nothing a modern reader would consider as evidence but made great play of *suspicion, infamy, loud insinuations* and *serious scandal which has arisen.* He writes that *the cardinals, archbishops and bishops ... abbots and the other prelates and procurators* listened to evidence together over several days, and that, as a result, four-fifths were firmly convinced *that the Order should be given an opportunity to defend itself and that it could not be condemned on the basis of the proof provided thus far.*

Given an 80% vote in their favour, the Templars might have anticipated being invited to offer a defence, or more likely for the accusations to be thrown out of court — but no. Clement ignores the views of his clergy and on his own account, by *ordinance and provision,* decides to suppress the order. His justification is that of avoiding scandal[1] and the financial imperative of disposing of the order's assets while they retained value.

Of course, there was no democracy in 14th century France but it does seem odd to ask a large gathering of clergy for their opinion and then ignore it, especially when so strongly expressed. Concerns over scandal and loss of financial value seem to have outweighed what the modern reader, and certainly the modern Freemason, would consider more important: justice and evidence.

To our eyes the most outrageous objection to allowing a defence comes in a letter from William Le Maire, Bishop of Angers, written in response to the invitation for submissions following the Council of Vienne. He submits that the Pope should disband the Order without any delay, *rejecting those ridiculous, calumnious allegations about the necessity for defence proceedings.*[2]

---

[1] By contrast, Pope Saint Gregory the Great (*c.*540-604) wrote: *It is better to allow the birth of scandal, than to abandon the truth.*

[2] *'Advice to the council of Vienne (April 1312)'*, William Le Maire, in Barber & Bate, *op. cit.* Is it unkind to mention his own opinion of his *somewhat limited intelligence*?

Understanding why Clement V did what he did is the key to understanding how and why the Templars were royally shafted, not only in our eyes but also in defiance of 14th century law.

Right to a defence

Henry Ansgar Kelly is clear that a defence was as much a right then as it is today. Accused of heresy, *anyone had a right to be defended by legal counsel, just like persons accused of other crimes. Only actual heretics, persons judicially convicted of heresy, were forbidden lawyers.*[1] Kelly is of the view that there was no church body known as the *Inquisition* (capital I) at the time, even if there were inquisitors (small i). In theory they all followed a procedure laid down by the Apostolic See, the fount of Roman Church authority.

He explains that an inquisition was one of two types of trial. On the one hand there were *civil actions* in civil courts where plaintiffs brought suits against defendants, much as today. A civil action was, and is, initiated by a plaintiff, a word dating back to the French *pleindre,* to complain or bewail. On the other hand, there were *inquisitions.* This ominous word actually comes from a tame verb, the Latin *inquisitio,* meaning to look into matters, often with a legal connotation, and the process was routine.

> *Used at all levels, from the courts of archdeacons and rural archpriests or deans charging rustics with fornication or adultery, to papally commissioned trials presided over by cardinals on charges brought against kings and queens.*[2]

An inquisition was initiated by public opinion, even rumour. A judge could instigate an inquisition only against someone who already had an infamous reputation, hence the rumours that Philip IV spread. A

---

[1] 'Inquisition and the Prosecution of Heresy: Misconceptions and Abuses', Henry Ansgar Kelly, *Church History*, December 1989.

[2] Kelly, *op. cit.* All Henry VIII's annulment trials were inquisitions.

judge had first to show that trustworthy members of the community considered the defendant guilty, and a defendant could prevent a trial by proving he had no such reputation. If an infamous reputation was proven, a trial would take place to decide whether the defendant's actions justified his notoriety. If he pleaded not guilty, the judge had to offer proof of guilt and the defendant had the right of defence. Kelly writes that the inquisition *was a brilliant and much-needed innovation in trial procedure.*

> *It served the generality of church courts very well and formed the basis of modern Continental criminal procedure. The abusive practices that came to prevail in the special heresy tribunals do not merit the name of inquisition but rather should be identified as a perversion of the inquisitorial process.*[1]

Crossfire

The Templars were caught in a crossfire between Pope Clement V and King Philip IV of France. It was during this crossfire that what were rumours in the bull *Vox in excelso* (22 March 1312) with its *suspicion, infamy, loud insinuations,* became facts five weeks later in the bull *Ad providam* (2 May) as *abominable, even unspeakable, deeds.* The background is a battle for religious supremacy between the throne and the papacy.

In 1302/3, the King had attempted to get Pope Boniface declared a heretic, and the Pope responded by excommunicating him. This somewhat resembles *l'affaire* Henry VIII. When the Pope declared his marriage to Anne Boleyn invalid, Henry responded by declaring the Pope no longer had any religious authority in England. The Pope excommunicated him and Parliament passed an act that Henry was head of a new Church of England. However, Philip did not seek to he head of the church but simply to have the Pope subservient to him.

---

[1] *Ibid.*

Boniface died a short while after this spat but when Clement V became Pope the fight was resumed. Philip's attack on the Templars was a tactic to put more pressure on the Pope. He had very juicy rumours spread about the Templar's behaviour, some new and some distortions of the truth. Runciman writes that Templars' *financial activities had brought them into close contact with the Moslems* and that many *had Moslem friends and took an interest in Moslem religion and learning.*[1] Innocent enough, until twisted to make them appear *collaborateurs*.

Clement, in an attempt to control the process, agreed to initiate an *inquisitio veritatis* (Kelly's *enquiry into the truth*). His intention was to dissipate the rumours, but he was clumsy. He informed the King of his intention on August 24, 1307, but being unwell at the time *he specified that the process would not begin before October.*[2] Philip pre-empted him and on 14 September commanded local justices to arrest all Templars in France.

Arrest and interrogation

On 22 September, Guillaume de Paris, the royal confessor and an inquisitor against heretical depravity,[3] followed up the King's letter with instructions to all his regional officers to hold the Templars under secure guard and to interrogate them with torture as necessary. On October 13, despite complaints from the Pope,[4] most Templars in France were arrested, including the Grand Master Jacques de Molay, then visiting from Cyprus.

---

[1] Runciman, *op. cit.*

[2] Demurger, *op. cit.*

[3] There is a difference between inquisition in general and inquisition against heresy. Bishops had jurisdiction over both; papal inquisitors only over the latter.

[4] *You have laid hands upon the persons and the goods of the Templars, and not just anyhow but going as far as imprisoning them, as though we were privy to the events.*

Arresting the members of a monastic order subject only to papal authority was not only illegal but in the worldview of the time, incomprehensible. The Pope was seen as a direct descendent from, and even the embodiment of St Peter, so the King's action was not far from arresting Christ's chosen apostle.[1] It also laid the King open to *severe vengeance at the final judgment*.[2]

The Royal interrogations commenced six days later. Victims were told that both the Pope and the King already knew all about their transgressions, that most Templars had already admitted the accusations were true, and that they would all be pardoned if they came clean, but tortured until death if not. Many, including Jacques de Molay, the Grand Master, 'confessed' to escape torture.

Admissions

It was not until August that a papal commission managed to hear confession from Templar leaders. The report of this commission, in what is now known as the *Chinon Parchment*, was discovered in 2001 by the Italian palaeographer, Barbara Frale, working in the Vatican archives.[3] It seems to bear out some of the accusations. A few brethren said that a brother had kissed them on the mouth when welcoming them, said to be common practice in early Christianity.[4]

Two Templars, inducted at the ages of sixteen and seventeen, said that they were taken aside by a brother holding a small cross under his cloak, who said: *You must denounce this one.* This may, of course, have been a test and Robert de Torville, Grand Prior of the Commandaries in England, said that at his induction he was several

---

[1] *Thou art Peter, and upon this rock I will build my church.* Matthew 16:18

[2] Bull *Omne Datum Optimum*, quoted earlier.

[3] 'The Chinon Chart: Papal absolution to the last Templar, Master Jacques de Molay,' Barbara Frale, *Journal of Medieval History*, 2004.

[4] As we saw above, when arriving in the Levant the excommunicated Frederick II was welcomed by the Templars but denied the usual kiss of peace.

times invited to denounce the figure on the cross, but steadfastly refused to do so. Whatever the case, the commission's finding was that the Templar initiation ceremony contained nothing improper, and so the Pope extended *the mercy of absolution* to the Order.

In the bull *Faciens misericordiam* Clement declared that the order and its leaders were reconciled with the Church, and that any power to judge them further was exclusively reserved to the Pope. He called for depositions from all Templars.

> *A veritable groundswell brought nearly six hundred brothers to the capital, the majority wishing to defend the Order and clear it of the accusations levelled against it.*[1]

The dodge

The royal court panicked until Archbishop Philippe de Marigny came up with a dodge. He proposed that anyone who confessed to personal transgressions when originally interrogated, but who then defended the Order before the papal commission, was thereby a *relapsed heretic* and liable to the death penalty. Clearly the two investigations had different purposes: the former to enquire whether an individual had sinned and the latter whether the institution was sinful. It is obvious that one may admit a personal sin while maintaining the innocence of the institution (and *vice versa*). The Archbishop either did not understand, or more likely deliberately ignored, the logic of this distinction.

Fifty-four Templars, caught by this dodge, were *relictus culiae saeculari* (released to the secular authority). The church maintained the fiction that it did not itself kill relapsed heretics; a fiction because *the civil authorities had no option but to proceed with the burning if they wanted to avoid a charge of harbouring and defending heretics.*[2]

---

[1] Demurger, *op. cit.*

[2] Frayling, *op.cit.*

Fiction or not, their burning at the stake was real.

The fix

The Pope gave up on the Knights Templar, and the shift from 'rumours' in *Vox in excelso* to 'facts' in *Ad providam* is a record of his concession. In the deal with Philip IV,

> he was offered the chance to preserve what, from his point of view, was the heart of the matter - the jurisdictional supremacy of the Apostolic See (even if this supremacy was only a facade).[1]

The Pope was being sandbagged. The Templars were toast whatever happened. The Pope had the choice of disbanding them himself and making it at least look like he was in charge, or seeing the King do it, thus admitting that Philip could override him. He chose the former to retain at least the shadow of his papal authority. In reality, Philip had demonstrated that the Pope danced to his tune.

The Templars were subjected to perpetual prohibition, which forbade anyone to enter the Order, wear its habit, or otherwise to act as a Templar. This was an announcement that the Pauperes commilitones Christi Templique Salomonici, the Poor Fellow Soldiers of Christ and the Temple of Solomon, no longer existed. The bull *Ad providam* transferred Templar property to the Hospitallers, at least preventing Philip getting his dirty hands on the money, and Clement delegated judgement of the Templars to three cardinals.

They sentenced them all to prison for life. Some accepted their fate, but Jacques de Molay and Geoffroi de Charney maintained their innocence, having confessed only under torture.[2] As relapsed

---

[1] 'A Heresy of State: Philip the Fair, the Trial of the *Perfidious Templars*, and the Pontificalisation of the French Monarchy', Julien Théry, *Journal of Medieval Religious Cultures*, 2013.

[2] 'Seven Papal Bulls and the Knights Templar', Peter L. Heineman, *St Mary the Virgin*, Sovereign Military Order of the Temple of Jerusalem, 2019.

heretics, they were burnt to death on the Ile aux Juifs, now underneath the Square du Vert Galant, west of the Pont-Neuf, where this plaque can be found.

Torture

Strange as it seems, there were rules governing the use of torture. Pope Innocent IV set them out in his 1252 CE bull *Ad extirpanda*.

> *The head of state or ruler must force all the heretics whom he has in custody, provided he does so without killing them or breaking their arms or legs ... to confess their errors and accuse other heretics whom they know, and specify their motives, and those whom they have seduced, and those who have lodged them and defended them.*

To force all heretics to confess their errors. Torture was to be used to make the victim 'confess' to a 'truth' already 'known'. Innocence was not an option. Victims were also tortured to make them accuse other heretics, *and those whom they have 'seduced', and those who have lodged them and defended them.* Even witnesses could be tortured if their initial evidence did not fit with what was 'known'.[1]

Torture was supposed to be used only once, but in practice it continued until the accused admitted his 'guilt'. The rules later restricted torture to the use of rods, switches or whips, excluding the rack, a restriction often ignored.

Truth, then and now

I have put several words into inverted commas because they mean quite the opposite of what they say. Today, we would ask for evidence of the accusations laid against the Templars. In a modern court of law, if an accusation cannot be proven beyond doubt the defendant is adjudged not guilty. However, we must again remember that *then* was very much *not* like *now*.

The truth of the accusation was what the church said and it was the inquisitor's job to get the victim to admit it. There was only one acceptable answer, and only on his giving that answer could the torture cease and the victim's eternal salvation and supernatural life be 'saved'. Eye-wash from beginning to end, agreed, but belief in the church was then unquestionably held. It spoke the word of God and was therefore right. Even today, what the Catholic Encyclopædia says of heresy smacks more of *then* than *now*.

> *The Church's legislation on heresy and heretics is often reproached with cruelty and intolerance. Intolerant it is: in fact its raison d'être is intolerance of doctrines subversive of the faith. Pertinacious adhesion to a doctrine contradictory to a point of faith clearly defined by the Church is heresy pure and simple, heresy in the first degree.*

---

[1] Kelly, *op. cit.*

142

Even if Kelly is right, that there was no such institution as an Inquisition in France, there certainly were many willing inquisitors. One fact emerging from studies on the psychology of torture is that it can be inflicted by people who are quite normal in their private lives. Christopher Browning's *Ordinary Men: reserve police battalion 101 and the final solution in Poland* is a chilling representation of this, as is Philip Zimbardo's *The Lucifer Effect; how good people turn evil*.[1]

Two Templars

Sean Field has carried out an analysis of extant documents, two from the *bailliage* of Rouen and three from the neighbouring *bailliage* of Caen, describing thirteen Templars who were living in five small *commanderies* in 1307. They were clearly not fighting men but managers of these small estates.

Porte sur la ville, Chateau de Caen.

Brother Gautier de Bullen, from the small Templar house at Voymer, was arrested on October 13. He was interrogated on two separate occasions on five articles:

1. *When first admitted to the order, had he been led to a secret place and shown the cross and crucifix and made three times to deny Jesus Christ and spit on the cross?*

2. *Had the brother carrying out the reception kissed him on the base of the spine, on the navel, and then on the mouth?*

3. *Had he been ordered to receive any brother who wanted to lie with him, since he was held to this by the statutes of the order?*

---

[1] The issue is discussed in West, *Goat*, *op. cit.*

4. *Had he ever participated in a chapter meeting in which an idol in the shape of a bearded head was venerated?*

5. *Did the priests of the order consecrate the Host as other priests were accustomed to do?*[1]

The required answer to each of these questions was 'Yes', but Brother Gautier twice answered 'No', or as the interrogators would have put it, he 'perjured'[2] himself twice. Told that *a third denial would not be tolerated,* an obvious threat of torture, he asked whether he could tell the 'truth' *without loss of body or members.* He was told that he could.

> *So Gautier, on bended knees and with tears streaming down his face, asked for the mercy of the church and of his own free will admitted that the first articles were true, but that he knew nothing about the charges concerning an idol or the priests' practices in celebrating the Mass. When they heard this admission,* [he was returned to] *the mercy of the church, and the knights, acting in the King's name, freed him of all corporal punishment.*[3]

Gautier de Bullens agreed the 'truth' of the accusations, only because he was threatened with torture. Four years after this, a Templar sergeant was asked about his own admission into the Order which had occurred some seventeen years earlier.

> *According to his testimony, the only other man admitted together with him that day was Gautier de Bullens, now identified by the blunt phrase 'burned at Paris.'*[4]

So Gautier had renounced his false confession and was burnt at the stake as *relapsed into heresy,* or as the Catholic Encyclopædia would

---

[1] 'Royal Agents and Templar Confessions in the *Bailliage* of Rouen', Sean L. Field, *French Historical Studies*, 2016.

[2] An odd use of *perjure.* When de Bullens denied the accusation, he was speaking the truth. When he accepted the 'truth' of the allegations, he was lying.

[3] Field, *op. cit.*

[4] Field, *op. cit.*

put it, he retained a *pertinacious adhesion to a doctrine contradictory to a point of faith clearly defined by the Church.*

Brother Guy Panaye (or Pesnée), the last of the thirteen, had also been interrogated twice, and had twice denied the accusations. Living as the only Templar at the small estate of Louvigny, he was not aware of the confessions of the other twelve, and on the third time of asking he again denied the accusations. He was then tortured, *suffering the punishment that the case required.* On the next day, being told of the other confessions, he gave in.

The stories of the other eleven are much the same as these two. Some died in prison; some revoked their confessions, and were burnt to death. None of these confessions would today be admissible in court, but *as the interrogators' own statements make clear, no brother was going to be allowed to escape without having confessed to the core of the charges.*[1] There are conflicting views on whether de Molay himself was tortured. The general consensus is that he was not. The threat of torture was enough to make him confess - at first. Perhaps unable to live with his betrayal of the Order, or perhaps fearing for his immortal soul, he reversed his confession.

English Templars

King Edward II at first refused to believe the accusations, so took no action until he received the papal bull *Pastoralis praeeminentiae* which *required all Christian princes to 'prudently, discreetly, and secretly'* arrest all Templars.[2] Two inquisitors arrived from France in September 1309, ready to examine English Templars. Two months later, getting nowhere, they sought permission to use torture.

---

[1] *Ibid.*

[2] Heineman, *op. cit.*

However, England *had developed a uniform legal machinery applying to all free men, which left no room for inquisitors.*[1] Complaining that *they could find no one to carry out torture properly,* and claiming that they had done everything they could, the two inquisitors left. It seems that few if any English Templars were tortured. The worst that accusers could prove was the crime of lay absolution, of laymen hearing confessions and absolving brethren. Even then,

> *William de la Forde, as preceptor of a house where the confession of the sick and aged made it of particular importance … said that lay preceptors absolved their brethren, not from mortal sin, but from acts of canonical disobedience … simply as an act of forgiveness, and that he believed the same was done in all Religious Orders.*[2]

A description of the arrests of Templars is available for all counties in which they had estates but in none have I found any mention of torture. A description of the events in York is perhaps the strongest.

> *Twenty-five Templars were placed in custody in York Castle and examined on the charge or heresy, idolatry, and other crimes, brought against the order by Pope Clement V and Philip IV of France. After a long-drawn-out trial, in which the evidence adduced against the knights was too flimsy to secure the desired conviction, a compromise was arrived at by which the brethren, without admitting their guilt, acknowledged that their order was strongly suspected of heresy.*[3]

---

[1] *The Trial of the Templars*, Malcolm Barber, Cambridge University Press, 1978.

[2] 'Houses of Knights Templars: Preceptory of Denney', *A History of the County of Cambridge and the Isle of Ely*, Vol. 2, ed. L F Salzman, Victoria County History, 1948.

[3] 'Houses of Knights Templar', *A History of the County of York*, Vol. 3, ed. William Page, Victoria County History, 1907.

Coda

If there is a theme to this book, it is that unity brings success and disunity, failure. This is as true today as it was then, as true in a masonic lodge as during the crusades. Unity requires selfless leadership, the root of the success of Zengī, Nur ad-Dīn, and Saladin. Unity was not much seen on the Christian side.

Viewed from today, the crusades are a sad tale of religious hatred, intolerance, racism, and violence. Such evils unfortunately remain common. Religion was a vehicle for evil back then and plays the same role all too often today. We may feel able to exempt the Templars from the very worst of these sins. They were accused of being too close to Islām and of having Muslim friends, accused of being too tolerant and insufficiently racist, and to the extent they lived up to their Rule, they may merit our esteem

It is, however, difficult to achieve an objective view of the Templars. The courage they certainly evinced may seem to us to have been squandered in a needless cause, in the brutal rejection of one set of non-rational beliefs by people committed to another. Both sides were promised eternal rewards. There is no evidence available in this life which, if either, reached that *undiscover'd country from whose bourn no traveller returns.*[1]

The place of religion in the Middle Ages was comprehensively different from its place today, and the Templars' embrace of a monastic vocation was far from exceptional. In 1200 CE there would have been about 18,500 nuns, monks and friars in England and Wales, accounting for half a percent of the population.[2] If that percentage were applied to today's population, there would be

---

[1] *Hamlet.*

[2] 'Clerical population of medieval England', Josiah Cox Russell, *Traditio*, Cambridge University Press, 1944.

250,000 nuns and monks, but in fact there are less than 7,000, just 0.014% of the population. Three quarters today are nuns,[1] compared with a tenth in 1200.[2] The difference between *then* and *now* is exemplified less mathematically in a passage from John Osborne's play *Luther*. Tetzel, the ecclesiastical huckster sells letters of pardon.

> *Not only am I empowered to give you these letters of pardon for the sins you've already committed, I can give you pardon for those sins you haven't even committed* (pause … then slowly) *but which you intend to commit.*

Satirical humour in a modern play, but reality in history. There was a Johann Tetzel, Grand Commissioner for indulgences in Germany. He did offer such outrageous pardons and people did buy them.

Crusading has long provided a basis for books, films and societies. Broadcaster Tony McMahon has counted 1,700 institutions styling themselves Templars. The most significant non-masonic order is perhaps the *Ordo Supremus Militaris Templi Hierosolymitani* (*Sovereign Military Order of the Temple of Jerusalem*), said to have consultative status with the United Nations, but all today's Templar bodies are of recent origin. None have any historical link to the order dissolved in 1312,[3] and one might note:

> *For the better part of a millennium after they ended, no one in Western Europe or the Middle East cared much about the crusades. The Christian world was more wrapped up in its Greek and Roman past, and when Muslim thinkers considered foreign invaders, they were more likely to remember the trauma of the Mongols.*[4]

---

[1] 'Monasteries in drive to recruit more novices', Gareth Rubin, *The Observer*, Jan 2009.

[2] *Medieval English Nunneries*, Eileen Power, Cambridge University Press, 1922.

[3] The supposed masonic link via the Rosslyn Chapel is comprehensively debunked in *The Rosslyn Hoax?* Robert L. D. Cooper, Lewis Masonic, 2006. Cooper is retired Curator of the Museum and Library of the Grand Lodge of Scotland.

[4] Nick Danforth, *Aljazeera America*, July 2014.

The existence of masonic orders which require a specific religious belief for admission has been questioned. From its very beginning, mainline Freemasonry has stood for the acceptance of any good man with a belief in a supreme being. In its early days, this meant accepting Jews and Catholics, unusual in a Hanoverian protestant society, but today it means accepting men and women[1] of all religions. Specific to the subject of this book, Freemasonry today welcomes Muslims and has many Muslim brothers.

The Provincial Prior of Essex, a valued
friend of the author.

---

[1] It is not often recognised that there are two orders of female Freemasons in the UK: the *Order of Women Freemasons* and *HFAF - Freemasonry for Women*. (HFAF refers to the latter's previous name: The Honourable Fraternity of Ancient Freemasons.)

In joining a Templar association today one should understand what the crusades really were. It is too easy to find the costumes, rituals and titles attractive while ignoring the intolerance and hatred that was an integral part of crusading.

There were a few notable exceptions, for example the odd friendship between Richard I and Saladin's brother al-Malik al-ʿĀdil; the understanding that Frederick II had with the Sulṭān al-Kāmil; and the insights of Islam acknowledged by old Levant hands. Perhaps such harmony and recognition should form part of the workings of masonic Knights Templar. While swearing to *act in the name of the Holy, Blessed and Glorious Trinity,* and to defend the Christian Faith, modern masonic Templars might also stand for open-mindedness towards all faiths, and against the bigotry that too often goes with religious belief.

For today's Templar, Urban II's misuse of the words of Jesus ought surely to give way to what is said in Matthew's Gospel. When asked for the greatest commandment of the law, Jesus replied:

> *Love the Lord your God with all your heart and with all your soul and with all your mind. This is the first and greatest commandment. And the second is like it: Love your neighbour as yourself. All the Law and the Prophets hang on these two commandments.*[1]

The Craft ritual certainly commends and even commands this.

---

[1] New International Version 22: 37-40.

The Long Closing in the First Degree

Brethren, remember that at the Master's pedestal you solemnly and voluntarily vowed to relieve and befriend with unhesitating cordiality every Brother who might need your assistance, that you have promised to remind him in the most gentle manner of his failings and to aid and vindicate his character whenever wrongfully traduced, to suggest the most candid, the most palliating and the most favourable circumstances, even when his conduct is justly liable to reprehension and blame. Thus shall the world see how dearly Freemasons love each other.

But, my Brethren, you are expected to extend these noble and generous sentiments still further. Let me impress upon your minds, and may it be instilled into your hearts, that every human creature has a just claim on your kind offices. I therefore trust that you will be good to all.

More particularly do I recommend to your care the household of the faithful, that by diligence and fidelity in the duties of your respective vocations, liberal beneficence and diffusive charity, by constancy and sincerity in your friendships; a uniformly kind, just, amiable and virtuous deportment, prove to the world the happy and beneficial effects of our ancient and honourable institution.

And particularly for Christian and Muslim Freemasons:

Let it not be said that you laboured in vain nor wasted your strength for nought; for your work is before the Lord and your recompense is with God. Finally Brethren, be of one mind, live in peace and may the God of love and mercy delight to dwell amongst you and bless you for evermore.

Bibliography

Aaron, David ed., *In their own words: voices of Jihad*, Rand Corporation, 2008.

Abulafia, Anna Sapir, 'The Abrahamic religions', *Discovering Sacred Texts*, British Library, 2019.

Addison, Charles G., *The History of the Knights Templar*, 1866, re-print Hardpress, 2013.

Adler, Marcus Nathan, *The Itinerary of Benjamin of Tudela*, Feldheim, 1907.

Allen, S.J. & Amy, Emilie, *The Crusades: a reader*, Univ. Toronto Press, 2104.

Amiran D.H.K, Arieh E, &Turcotte T, 'Earthquakes in Israel and adjacent areas', *Israel Exploration Journal*, 1994.

Ammianus Marcellinus

   The Roman History, trnsl. George D. Yonge, Bell, 1911.

   Ammianus Marcellinus, Rolfe, John C., Loeb Classical Library, 1935.

Anon., *Chronique d'Ernoul et Bernard le Trésorier* c.1230, ed. Count Louis de Mas Latrie, Société de l'histoire de France, 1871.

Asbridge, Thomas, *The Crusades*, Simon & Schuster, 2010.

Augustine (Saint), *Contra Faustum Manichaeum*, tr. Richard Stathert, in Philip Schaff ed. *The Nicene and Post-Nicene Fathers*, Hendrickson, 1994.

Bacon, Francis, *Of Holy War*, 1622, in *The Works of Francis Bacon*, Vol. 3, ed. James Spedding, Robert Leslie Ellis & Douglas Denon Heath, Cambridge University Press, 2011.

Bahā' ad-Dīn, *The rare and excellent history of Saladin*, trnsl. D.S. Richards, Ashgate Publishing, 2002.

Baker, Simon, *Ancient Rome: The Rise and Fall of an Empire*, BBC Books, 2007.

Barber, Malcolm, *The New Knighthood*, Cambridge University Press, 1994, *The Trial of the Templars*, Cambridge University Press, 1978.

   The Templars, ed. & trnsl. with Keith Bate, Manchester Univ. Press, 2002.

      'Advice to the council of Vienne,' William *Le Maire*

      'The anger and the sorrow of a Templar in the Holy Land,' poem, Ricaut Bonomel.

      'Carriage of pilgrims from Marseille.'

      '*De constructione castri Saphet,*' anon.

      'Deposit of jewels by James I of Aragon at Monzón.'

      'Gathering crusading taxes.'

      'Inquest of the Templar lands in Essex.'

      'The pilgrimage of Pons Lautier of Colonzelle.'

'Pope Honorius III orders the prelates of Sicily to protect the Hospitallers and Templars.'

Benedict the Pole., *Ystoria Mongalorum*, trnsl. William Woodville Rockhill, *The Journey of William of Rubruck*, 1900, reprint Forgotten Books.

Bennett, Matthew, 'La Régle du Temple as a Military Manual or How to Deliver a Cavalry Charge,' *Studies in Mediaeval History Presented to R. Allen Brown*, ed. Christopher Harper-Bill, Christopher J. Holdsworth, & Janet L. Nelson, Boydell, 1989.

Bernard (Saint), *Liber ad milites Templi: De laude novae militae*, ed. Conrad Greenia, ORD Online Encyclopædia.

Bird, Jessalynn; Peters, Edward; Powell, James M. (eds) *Crusade and Christendom: Annotated Documents in Translation from Innocent III to the Fall of Acre*, 1187-1291, University of Pennsylvania Press, 2017.

'The capture of Damietta.'

'Clamat in Auribus.'

'The Crusade of Frederick II.'

'How a great stir was made at this time to assist in the crusade.'

'Ibn Wasil on Louis's defeat and captivity.'

'Jerusalem is handed over to the Franks.'

'The road to Acre.'

'Recruiting sermon.'

'The Rhineland Crusaders.'

Boas, Adrian J., *Crusader Archeology*, Routledge, 1999.

Borton, Major N. R. M., 'The 14th Army in Burma: A Case Study in Delivering Fighting Power,' *Defence Studies*, Autumn 2002.

Broadhurst, R.J.C. & Irwin, Robert, *The travels of Ibn Jubayr*, Bloomsbury, 2019.

Browne, Edward G., *A Literary History of Persia*, Cambridge University Press, 1902, reprint 2009.

Browning, Christopher, *Ordinary Men: reserve police battalion 101 and the final solution in Poland*, Harper, 2017.

Brundage, James, *The Crusades: A Documentary History*, Marquette University Press, 1962.

'Pope Innocent III, Epistle 136'.

'Description of the Holy Land and of the way thither'.

Cobb, Paul M., *The Race for Paradise*, Oxford University Press, 2014.

Condliffe, Jamie, 'The napalm of Byzantium,' *New Scientist*, Feb 2021.

Conrad, Sarah Evers, 'Horse Feeding Basics,' *The Horse*, December 2019.

Cooper, Robert L.D., *The Rosslyn Hoax?*, Lewis Masonic, 2006.

Danforth, Nick, 'The enduring influence of the Crusades,' *Aljazeera America*, July 2014.

Davis Paul K., *100 Decisive Battles*, Oxford University Press, 2001.

Davis, William Stearns, *A Short History of the Near East, from the Founding of Constantinople*, Reprint Ulan Press, 2012.

Demurger, Alain, *The Last Templar*, trnsl. Antonia Nevill, Profile Books, 2004.

Eaves, Peter, 'Crusader Castles in the Holy Land,' Wednesday Talk, 11 September 2016, *Museum of the Order of St John*.

Edbury, Peter W., *The Conquest of Jerusalem and the Third Crusade, sources in translation*, Ashgate Publishing 1998.

'Letter to Archumbald'.

Ellenblum, Ronnie, *Frankish Rural Settlement in the Latin Kingdom of Jerusalem*, Cambridge University Press, 1998.

Ferris, Eleanor, 'The Financial Relations of the Knights Templar to the English Crown,' *American Historical Review*, October 1902.

Field, Sean L., 'Royal Agents and Templar Confessions in the *Bailliage* of Rouen,' *French Historical Studies*, 2016.

Fleury, Claude, *Catechisme Historique*, 1683, quoted in Jortin, John.

Forey, Alan, 'Notes on Templar personnel and government,' *Journal of Medieval History, 2009*.

Frale, Barbara, 'The Chinon chart: Papal absolution to the last Templar, Master Jacques de Molay,' *Journal of Medieval History*, 2004.

Frayling, Christopher, *Strange Landscape*, BBC Books, 1995.

Gabrieli, Francesco, *Arab Historians of the Crusades*, trnsl. E.J. Costello, Routledge, 1969.

Geoffrey of Villehardouin, *Chronicle of the Fourth Crusade and the Conquest of Constantinople*, trnsl. Frank T. Marzials, J.M. Dent, 1908.

Gershon, Livia, 'Chivalry Was Established to Keep Thuggish, Medieval Knights in Check,' *History.com*, January 2019.

Gibb, Sir Hamilton, *The Life of Saladin*, The Clarendon Press, 1973.

Gibbon, Edward, *The History of the Decline and Fall of the Roman Empire*, ed. David Womersly, Penguin, 2000.

Grinberg, Mariya, 'Wartime Commercial Policy & Trade between Enemies,' *International Security*, 2021.

Gunter of Pairis, *Hystoria Constantinopolitana*, ed. & trnsl. Alfred J. Andrea, University of Pennsylvania Press, 2021.

Halsall, Paul, *Barbarian Migrations and the Roman West 376-568*, Cambridge University Press, 2007.

'Medieval Sourcebook: Urban II,' *History Sourcebooks Project*, Fordham University.

Hamilton, Bernard, *Monastic Reform, Catharism, and the Crusades 900-1300*, Variorum, 1979.

with Jotischky, Andrew, *Latin and Greek Monasticism in the Crusader States*, Cambridge University Press, 2020.

Heineman, Peter L. 'Seven Papal Bulls and the Knights Templar,' *St Mary the Virgin*, Sovereign Military Order of the Temple of Jerusalem, 2019.

Herrin Judith, *Byzantium: The Surprising Life of a Medieval Empire*, Princeton University Press, 2009.

Hosler, John D., *The Siege of Acre 1189-1191*, Yale University Press, 2018.

Hume, David, *The History of England*, 1778, reprint The Liberty Fund.

Ibn al-Athīr, *Perfect History* ed. D.S. Richards, Routledge, 2006.

Imā-ad-Dīn, writings collected in *Le Livre des Deux Jardins*, 1898, trnsl. Charles Barbier de Maynard, reprinted Hachette Livre-BNF, 2018.

Jenott, Lance, *Silk Road Seattle*, Simpson Center for the Humanities at the University of Washington.

John of Würzberg, *Description of Jerusalem*, trnsl. Aubrey Stewart, Palestine Pilgrims Text Society 1890, reprint Alpha Editions, 2019.

John of Pian, *The Journey of Friar John of Pian de Carpine to the Court of Kuyuk (Güyüg) Khan*, 1245-1247, trnsl. William Woodville Rockhill, in *The Journey of William of Rubruck*, 1900, Hakluyt Society, reprint Forgotten Books.

Jones, Dan, 'What the Far Right Gets Wrong About the Crusades,' *Time*, October 10, 2019.

Jortin, John, *Remarks on Ecclesiastical History*, 1805, reprint BiblioBazaar, 2009.

Juvayni, Atâ-Malek, *Tarīkh-i Jahān-gushā*, trnsl. J.A. Boyle as *Genghis Khan: A History of the World Conqueror*, Univ. of Washington Press , 1997.

Kelly, Henry Ansgar, 'Inquisition and the Prosecution of Heresy: Misconceptions and Abuses,' *Church History*, December 1989.

Krey August C. ed., *The First Crusade: Accounts of Eyewitnesses and Participants*, reprint Forgotten Books, 2016.

'Dei gesta per Francos.'

'Chronicle of First Crusade.'

'History of Jerusalem.'

Kuniholm, Peter, 'Wood,' *Oxford Encyclopedia of Archaeology in the Near East*, ed. Eric M. Meyers, Oxford University Press, 1997.

155

Latrie, Count Louis de Mas, *Chronique d'Ernoul et Bernard le Trésorier, (c.1230)*, Société de l'histoire de France, 1871.

Lloyd, Simon, *English Society and the Crusade*, Clarendon Press, 1988.

Maalouf, Amin, *The crusades through Arab eyes*, Saqi Books, 1984.

Mackintosh-Smith, Tim, *The Arabs*, Yale University Press, 2019.

Madden, Thomas,

'Crusade Myths,' *Catholic Dossier*, 2002.

The Crusades Controversy: Setting the Record Straight, The Dynamic Catholic Institute, 2017.

Maher Abu-munshar, 'Sultan al-Kamil, Emperor Frederick II and the Submission of Jerusalem,', *International Journal of Social Science and Humanity*, September 2013.

Mango, Cyril, ed. *The Oxford History of Byzantium*, Oxford University Press, 2002.

McClary, Richard, 'Craftsmen in Medieval Anatolia: Methods and Mobility,' *Architecture and Landscape in Medieval Anatolia, 1100-1500*, ed. Patricia Blessing, & Rachel Goshgarian, Edinburgh Univ. Press, 2017.

McNeill, Tom, *English Heritage Book of Castles*, English Heritage, 1992.

Menache, Sophia,

Clement V, Cambridge University Press, 1998.

'The Templar Order: a failed ideal?' *The Catholic Historical Review*, January 1993.

Mendola, Luigi, 'Was Frederick II an atheist?' *Best of Sicily Magazine*, 2012.

Mills, Charles, *The History of the Crusades*, Longman, 1821, reprint Forgotten Books, 2016.

Mitchell, P.D., 'The spread of disease with the crusades,' *Between Text & Patient: Medical Enterprise in Medieval & Early Modern Europe*, ed. B. Nance & E.F. Glaze, KT, 2011.

Morelle, Rebecca, 'Richard the Lionheart's mummified heart analysed,' *BBC News*, 28 February 2013.

Mourad, Suleiman, *The Conversation*, July 9, 2018.

Murray, Alan. V., *The Crusader Kingdom of Jerusalem: A Dynastic History, 1099-1124*, Oxford Unit for Prosopographical Research, 2000.

Mylod, Elizabeth J., *Latin Christian Pilgrimage in the Holy Land, 1187-1291*, University of Leeds, 2013.

Norwich, John Julius, (2nd Viscount Norwich), *Byzantium, the early centuries*, Guild Publishing, 1989.

Oakeshott, Ewart

    A Knight and his Armour, Dufour, 2nd edition, 1999.

    A Knight and his Horse, Dufour, 1999.

Painter, Sidney, 'The Third Crusade: Richard the Lionhearted and Philip Augustus,' in *A History of the Crusades*, Volume II, ed. Robert Lee Wolff & Harry W. Hazard, University of Wisconsin Press, 1969.

Paris, Matthew, *Chronica Major,* ed. Henry Richards Luard, Cambridge University Press, 2012.

Partner, Peter, *The Knights Templar and their Myth*, Press, 1981.

Perkins, Clarence, 'The Wealth of the Knights Templars in England,' *American Historical Review*, 1910.

Pèlerin Richard le, *Chanson d'Antioche, c.*1190, ed. Jeanne Paule Beaupoil Marquise de Sainte-Aulaire, Didier et Ce. 1862.

Phillips, Jonathan

    'The Crusades,' *History Today,* 2015.

Power, Eileen, *Medieval English Nunneries*, Cambridge Univ. Press, 1922.

Prawer, Joshua, 'The settlement of the Latins in Jerusalem,' *Speculum*, 1952.

Pringle, Denys, 'Architecture in the Latin East,' *The Oxford History of the Crusades*, ed. Jonathan Riley-Smith, Oxford University Press, 1999.

Procopius, *The Gothic Wars*, trnsl. H.B. Dewing, Loeb, 1919.

Puckett, Jaye, 'Reconmenciez novele estoire: The Troubadours and the Rhetoric of the Later Crusades,' *MLN*, 2001.

Ralph of Coggeshall, *Chronicon Anglicanum,* Google e-book.

Riley-Smith, Jonathan, ed. *The Oxford History of the Crusades*, Oxford University Press, 1999.

    'Introduction,' Jonathan Riley-Smith.

    'Islam and the crusades, 1096-1699,' Robert Irwin.

    'The Military Orders,' Alan Forey.

Rossabi, Morris, *The Mongols*, Oxford University Press, 2012.

Rubin, Gareth, 'Monasteries in drive to recruit more novices,' Gareth Rubin, *The Observer*, January 2009.

Runciman, Steven, *History of the Crusades*, Cambridge University Press, three volumes, 1952-1954.

Russell, Josiah Cox, 'Clerical population of medieval England,' *Traditio,* Cambridge University Press, 1944.

Saewulf, 'Travels,' in *Early Travels in Palestine*, ed. Thomas Wright, 1848, reprint Cosimo Classics, 2011.

Sarris, Peter, *Byzantium*, Oxford University Press, 2015.

Schaff, Philip ed., *The Nicene and Post-Nicene Fathers*, Hendrickson, 1994. 'Contra Faustum Manichaeum,' trnsl. Richard Stathert.

Scott, Sir Walter, *Essays on Chivalry, Romance and the Drama*, Adam & Charles Black, 1870, reprint Forgotten Books, 2016.

Sobchack, Vivian, 'Chasing the Maltese Falcon: on the fabrications of a film prop,' *Journal of Visual Culture*, 2007.

Southern, Richard William, *The Making of the Middle Ages*, Pimlico, 1993.

Spencer, Stephen J., 'The Third Crusade in historiographical perspective,' *History Compass*, July 2021.

Théry, Julien, 'A Heresy of State: Philip the Fair, the Trial of the *Perfidious Templars*, and the Pontificalisation of the French Monarchy,' *Journal of Medieval Religious Cultures*, 2013.

Tyerman, Christopher

> *The Debate on the Crusades*, Manchester University Press, 2011.
>
> *God's War*, Penguin, 2007.
>
> *How to Plan a Crusade: Reason and Religious War in the High Middle Ages*, Penguin, 2015.

Upton-Ward, *The Rule of the Templars*, Boydell Press, 1992.

Victoria County Histories, online at www.british-history.ac.

Villehardouin, Geoffrey, *Chronicle of the Fourth Crusade and the Conquest of Constantinople*, trnsl. Frank T. Marzials, J.M. Dent, 1908.

Voltaire, Francois-Marie Arouet, *An Essay on Universal History: the manners and spirit of nations*, 1756, trnsl. Peter Constantine, reprint, HardPress, 2018.

Vryonis, Speros, *Byzantium and Europe*, Harcourt, Brace, 1967.

West, David

> *Deism at the time of the founders of the Premier Grand Lodge*, Hamilton House, 2018.
>
> *The Goat, the Devil and the Freemason*, Hamilton House, 2013.
>
> *Masonic Legends*, Hamilton House, 2017.

William of Tyre, *Historia rerum in partibus transmarinis gestarum*, A History of Deeds done beyond the Sea, trnsl. Emily Atwater Babcock & A. C. Krey, Columbia University Press, 1943.

Wilson, Colonel Sir Charles William, *The pilgrimage of the Russian Abbott Daniel in the Holy Land*, Palestine Pilgrims' Text Society, 1888.

Wollock, Jennifer Goodman, *Rethinking Chivalry and Courtly Love*, Praeger Series on the Middle Ages, 2011.

Young, Alan, *Tudor and Jacobean Tournaments*, Sheridan House, 1987.

Zimbardo, Philip, *The Lucifer Effect; how good people turn evil*, Rider, 2008.

Illustrations